The Embedded Librarian

Innovative Strategies for Taking Knowledge Where It's Needed

David Shumaker

 **Information Today, Inc.**
Medford, New Jersey

First Printing, 2012

The Embedded Librarian: Innovative Strategies for Taking Knowledge Where It's Needed

Library of Congress Cataloging-in-Publication Data

Shumaker, David, 1950-
    The embedded librarian : innovative strategies for taking knowledge where it's needed / David Shumaker.
        p. cm.
    Includes bibliographical references and index.
    ISBN 978-1-57387-452-6
    1. Reference services (Libraries). 2. Libraries and institutions. 3. Librarians--Professional relationships. 4. Librarians--Effect of technological innovations on. 5. Teams in the workplace. I. Title.
    Z711.S38 2012
    025.5'2--dc23

                                                                2012017662

Printed and bound in the United States of America

Editor-in-Chief and Publisher: John B. Bryans
VP Graphics and Production: M. Heide Dengler
Project Editor: Marydee Ojala
Cover Designer: Danielle Nicotra

www.infotoday.com

The research that forms the foundation of this book was supported in part by a grant from the Special Libraries Association. The Special Libraries Association does not necessarily support any of the findings or conclusions presented in the book.

For
Suzannah Alice

Contents

PART 2: Your Path to Success 121

Acknowledgments

This book has been written in less than a year, but the idea for it has been germinating for much longer. Among the many people who have guided, taught, influenced, and encouraged me along the way are, in chronological order:

My colleagues in Information Services at the MITRE Corporation, whose amazing professionalism first showed me the potential of embedded librarianship.

Dr. Martha Hale, former dean of the School of Library and Information Science at the Catholic University of America, who gave me a chance to become a full-time faculty member and encouraged me to pursue a research theme that interested me.

Laura Tyler, who proposed a research project on embedded librarianship and co-authored the first "Embedded Library Services" paper.

Mary Talley, my co-investigator for the Special Libraries Association (SLA) Models of Embedded Librarianship research grant, whose insight, high standards, and inexhaustible energy were essential to the project's successful outcome.

Judy Siess, who planted the idea of writing a book on embedded librarianship in a conversation at the 2009 SLA Conference and whose *Searcher* article captures the essence of the model.

Marydee Ojala, editor of this work, who has encouraged and guided me through the proposal and writing process. Marydee has perfected the art of being demanding and supportive at the same time.

And above all, my long-suffering family, especially my wife, Donna—friend and advisor, partner and collaborator.

About the Blog

www.embeddedlibrarian.com

Want to know more? Want to join the conversation? The Embedded Librarian blog, at www.embeddedlibrarian.com, features posts by the author on all matters related to embedded librarianship. New research, interesting updates, and musings on successes and challenges are all part of the mix—it's the only blog dedicated to embedded librarianship, covering all aspects of this important trend.

Foreword

Imagine a librarian accompanying you throughout the course of your day.

You drive to work, and the librarian is in the car with you, telling you the latest news and helping you avoid traffic jams. You leave your office to get lunch and the librarian walks down the street with you, describing the specials at your favorite restaurants. You go home and sit down to eat, and the librarian is there at the table with you, telling you how the stock market performed that day.

Sound far-fetched or strange? It shouldn't. Librarians historically have been gateways to information, and today we carry pocket-sized and paper-sized librarians around with us wherever we go. We call them different names—smartphones, tablets, netbooks, and so on—but we use them to access information, just as we would a librarian.

With so much information available at the touch of a telephone or computer screen, librarians must identify and embrace new roles to provide value to their organizations and customers. One path that holds promise is to *partner with groups of information users*—be they college students working on a class project, scientists conducting drug trials in a laboratory, attorneys researching a difficult court case, or architects designing a new home—to help them gain a competitive advantage. Librarians who follow this path *participate in information communities* and share responsibility for their success or failure. They *develop relationships with team members* and identify information sources, programs, and channels that will *enhance the team's performance*.

This approach, known as embedded librarianship, isn't new—it has its roots in the health care field of the 1960s, when librarians began to join doctors and nurses as they visited hospital patients and discussed their status and treatment. What *is* new is that research has identified the characteristics of successful embedded librarians and illuminated the practices and principles that enable these librarians to exceed their colleagues' expectations and add value to their work.

This research has been led by Dave Shumaker, who has spent the past 3-plus years studying embedded librarian programs to determine the criteria that define them, the indicators of their success, and their methods of operation and evaluation. With financial help through a grant from the Special Libraries Association, Dave has traveled to several organizations with embedded programs and conducted interviews and focus groups with librarians and their clients. By analyzing the information he obtained and comparing embedded programs that have thrived over time with those that haven't, Dave has developed insights into the nature of embedded librarianship and discerned how it can best serve the interests of organizations and librarians alike.

Now, in *The Embedded Librarian: Innovative Strategies for Taking Knowledge Where It's Needed*, Dave makes a compelling argument for a model of librarianship based on community, flexibility, accountability, relevance, and responsibility. Using information gleaned from a thorough literature review as well as interviews and his own observations, Dave explains why librarians need to transcend their traditional role of fulfilling information transactions and replace it with a strategy that focuses on developing relationships with teams and becoming immersed in their projects and activities. In this model, librarianship ceases to be seen (and practiced) as a service to individuals and instead is recognized as fundamental to the ongoing work of the organization and its units.

As CEO of the Special Libraries Association, I have seen embedded librarianship evolve from an innovative concept being practiced by a handful of librarians to an accepted strategy for demonstrating the value of our profession. I recommend *The Embedded Librarian* to information professionals of all ages and in all settings, and to their managers and organizational leaders as well. In a global economy where the most successful organizations are often those that make the best use of information, embedding librarians into work teams can reap significant dividends.

Janice R. Lachance,
chief executive officer,
Special Libraries Association

Introduction

Two beliefs form the foundation of this book.

The first is nothing new: *Librarianship is changing, and must change.* I don't know anyone in the profession who doesn't believe this. The way society handles recorded information is undergoing the greatest change in centuries (since Gutenberg, in Western society), and we're likely to continue to experience accelerating change for the foreseeable future. The mutually reinforcing revolutions in our tools and our social structures have fundamental implications for the profession of librarianship that we are in the midst of working through.

The second is not so widely discussed nor accepted: *Librarians in all sectors of the profession must change in fundamentally similar ways.* In the course of studying embedded librarianship and doing research for this book, I've been struck that the profession of librarianship is very disconnected and stovepiped. We don't talk to one another much, and we don't seem to recognize that we stand on common ground—and need to travel, together, in the same direction. Many in the American Library Association talk as if *library* was synonymous with *public library*; they don't seem to recognize that librarians work in other sectors, even outside traditional library structures and organizations, and especially in the private sector. Medical librarians have done amazing work, but it's all written up in the medical library journals, and if you're not a medical librarian reading those journals, you probably haven't read about it. School media specialists are fighting a desperate battle to change the image of school librarianship and get educators to recognize its importance, but like the medical librarians, they're isolated from other segments of the profession. Meanwhile, some members of the Special Libraries Association are so alienated from librarianship, which they perceive as being stuck in both the stereotypes and the habits of the past, that they've tried to take any reference to libraries or librarians out of the association's name.

Certainly, there are important differences among the sectors. However, the premise of this book is that the natures of the changes that are taking place—and must take place—are similar. We librarians must master new technologies for managing and delivering information. We must engage with knowledge and recognize the difference between information and knowledge. We must develop new organizational structures and new management techniques. Above all, we must establish new relationships with *information users*—the people in our communities, universities, schools, corporations, agencies, and firms who need us. These imperatives are operating in every sector of the profession.

This book focuses on those new relationships. It surveys and analyzes the fundamental redefinition of the relationship between librarians and the communities in which they work. The name given to this change is *embedded librarianship*. Part 1 of this book presents the *what* and the *why*, while Part 2 addresses the *how to*.

Part 1 focuses on the nature and status of embedded librarianship. Chapter 1 defines it and provides some examples of the ways it is changing the role of the librarian in different settings. Chapter 2 relates the growth of embedded librarianship to larger social and economic trends and offers an explanation of its advantages. Chapters 3 through 6 survey its development in higher education, health sciences, specialized organizations such as corporations and government agencies, and schools and public libraries.

Part 2 shifts the focus to practices of successful embedded librarians—practices for preparing, initiating, sustaining, and evaluating embedded librarianship. Drawing on the available research findings, it presents a series of exercises from workshops that I have given on three continents (North America, Australia and Oceania, and Africa). The objective is to provide tools that any librarian can adapt and apply to local circumstances. Chapter 7 offers a self-assessment methodology that can help a librarian explore whether conditions are favorable for initiating or expanding embedded librarianship. Chapter 8 continues the process to the steps for introducing embedded librarianship. Chapter 9 discusses the challenges of sustaining it for the long term, and Chapter 10 specifically discusses methods for evaluating embedded librarianship, demonstrating its value (or making corrections as needed!) and communicating the results to the appropriate stakeholders.

The primary audience for the book is anyone who considers herself or himself a librarian. Regardless of the sector you work in, regardless of whether you are in school or have been in the profession for 30 years, I hope you'll find something of value in these pages. You may already be an embedded librarian, or the concept may be brand new to you. Whether your title is reference librarian, library media specialist, information analyst, or any of the dozens of other job titles that librarians use—if librarianship is part of you and you want to develop your professional role—then I hope this book will give you a new idea, point the way forward, and help you develop your knowledge, sharpen your techniques, and advance your career.

And when you've finished the book, I invite you to join the conversation. If you're persuaded that this is an important topic, if you have questions or comments, if you'd like to share your own experiences or just keep up with what others are doing and saying, then come visit my blog at www.embeddedlibrarian.com. I look forward to seeing you there!

PART

Embedded Librarianship
Yesterday, Today, and Tomorrow

Part 1 of the book explores the phenomenon of embedded librarianship.

It starts by clarifying the terminology. Different sectors of librarianship do not share a common vocabulary for this innovation. Librarians have used the term in different ways—and they have used other terms for fundamentally similar initiatives. Chapter 1 adopts a definition of embedded librarianship that is broad enough to unify the practices among different professional groups, while maintaining a sharp distinction from the practices of traditional librarianship. It also explores the idea that there are degrees of embedded librarianship—it is not an all-or-nothing proposition. Furthermore, it differentiates what is meant by embedded librarianship, apart from other innovations taking place in the profession.

Chapter 2 considers why embedded librarianship has arisen, why it has grown, and why it is a promising direction for the future. Chapter 2 makes the case that embedded librarianship is not only here to stay but also likely to continue growing. The reasons for this are both *push* and *pull*. Push means that the old model of library service is breaking down—the profession is being pushed to find new approaches. Pull means that important trends in society and the workplace are beckoning—inviting librarians to align with them. We explore these trends as presented in the works of Peter Drucker, Thomas Friedman, Thomas Davenport, Laurence Prusak, Daniel Pink, Scott Page, and a few others.

Chapters 3 through 6 constitute a survey of embedded librarianship across the major organizational sectors in which librarians work. Chapter 3 begins the survey with a focus on librarians in higher education. It traces the origins of embedded librarianship in the liaison librarian concept, reviews the importance of the librarian's role in information literacy instruction, and presents emerging roles for librarians in curriculum development and the research mission of the university. Chapter 4 shifts to the health sciences field, whose clinical medical librarian programs initiated in the 1970s are the earliest examples of embedded librarianship. In the succeeding decades, medical librarians have continued to develop their role, while also engaging in more thorough evaluation than have librarians in any other sector. Chapter 5 reviews the status of embedded librarianship in other specialized settings, such as corporations, law firms, and government agencies. Chapter 6 concludes Part 1 by showing how the teacher librarians of primary and secondary education are embodying the idea of embedded librarianship and how public library staff members are building partnerships and networking throughout the communities they serve in a way that has much in common with the embedded model.

Upon completing Part 1, you should have a good grasp of embedded librarianship: what it is, why it is important, and how it is growing in every sector of librarianship. Then you'll be ready for Part 2, in which you'll be able to apply your knowledge to your own workplace.

Chapter 1

Defining Embedded Librarianship

Try this experiment. Stand on a street corner and ask passersby what they think a librarian is or does. Chances are you'll hear a lot of answers that come down to this: A librarian is someone who works in a library. For centuries, librarians were identified with the buildings in which they worked. Most people don't differentiate between library workers with master's degrees and those without, or between librarians doing public services and those doing technical services work. For all of recorded history, librarians have worked in libraries. Long after we unchained our books, opened up our stacks, and encouraged people to take materials out of our libraries, we have continued to confine ourselves inside our libraries.

Today, that's changing. Digital information is ubiquitous. People don't have to come into libraries to get it or to use it. They obtain and use information at home, in the office, in dorm rooms, and in restaurants. They gather information sitting down and standing up. They use desktops and laptops, smartphones and tablets. Moreover, they access every type of information this way—whether it's for business, personal interest, scholarship, or science. Thus, when people *do* come to a library, they don't come for the traditional reasons. They come for programs, a quiet place to work, group study spaces, or to use the computers. They don't come to ask for help from the reference librarians, and as a result, traditional reference activity is declining. Smart librarians have recognized this trend. In fact, they've realized that the new environment of abundant, ubiquitous information offers them the opportunity to rethink traditional library services and do work that is new, more challenging, more rewarding, and more valuable for their communities.

Initiatives to let the librarians out of the libraries and create new modes of librarianship are taking various forms. Roving librarians wander the stacks to look for people who might like some help with their research, or they set up shop in student centers and dormitories to offer assistance with term papers and other assignments. Their motto is "Have laptop, will

3

travel." Some academic institutions designate *personal librarians*, who help students with information problems just as academic advisors give advice on academic courses and programs. Some authors advocate that librarians become "consultants"—on-call experts who can apply their expertise on demand to meet the information needs of any and all clients.

Definition of an Embedded Librarian

Perhaps the most succinct definition of the term *embedded librarian* is the one offered by Jezmynne Dene (2011). Describing her experiences with the initiation of embedded librarianship at the Claremont Colleges, Dene noted that "we chose to define an embedded librarian as 'an integral part to the whole,' based on the geological definition of an embedded element" (p. 225).

This brief definition captures the essence of the concept. Embedded librarianship is a distinctive innovation that moves the librarians out of libraries and creates a new model of library and information work. It emphasizes the importance of forming a strong working relationship between the librarian and a group or team of people who need the librarian's information expertise. As the relationship develops, the librarian's knowledge and understanding of the group's work and objectives grow, which leads in turn to greater alertness to the information and knowledge needs of the group. The embedded librarian becomes just as engaged in the work of the team as any other team member. As the engagement grows, the embedded librarian develops highly customized, sophisticated, and value-added contributions to the team—contributions that sometimes go far beyond the confines of traditional library reference work and that some might be surprised to find a librarian delivering. The librarian functions as a team member like any other—and shares responsibility for team and organizational outcomes with all the other members of the team.

These points deserve elaboration. In traditional reference service—whether it's performed at a reference desk or virtually, by phone, email, or text messaging—librarians typically provide library users with an answer, advice, or instructional tips and guidance on research methods. The librarians' responsibility ends there. Librarians need not understand the library user's project or ultimate objective in any great detail; in fact, some library service guidelines treat inquiring about the information seeker's intent as an invasion of privacy. The philosophy of embedded librarianship is quite different. Embedded librarians need to be fully "read into" the nature of the work being performed. Whether it's the learning outcomes of an academic course or the commercial objectives of a market research study, embedded librarians need a full understanding of the nature of the task and the goals of the effort.

In traditional reference work, the operating assumption is that all librarians are interchangeable. The patron is supposed to deal with the librarian on duty at the desk at any given time, and the librarians are expected to deliver consistent service regardless of the nature of the request. Relationships can form, but they aren't actively fostered. Embedded librarians, on the other hand, deliberately build relationships—with faculty, with students, with the marketing department, with a research and development team, or with any other user group. It's an important part of their work because that's how their understanding grows. The relationships and the understanding of the work are the prerequisites that enable the librarians to customize contributions to the team's work and provide sophisticated, highly valued information management and information services.

In traditional reference service, librarians are responsible for good reference work, period. They generally don't have any way to know how their work affects the work of their patron, apart from the occasional thank-you note—which usually praises only their efficient and pleasant service and rarely cites the impact of the work. However, the close engagement that forms between embedded librarians and the information user teams they work with naturally leads to the librarian's assuming the role of team member rather than traditional standalone service provider. As team members, embedded librarians take on the same responsibility for team outcomes that other members share. Embedded librarians often go above and beyond traditional expectations in contributing to the team's success.

Figure 1.1 depicts the factors that define embedded librarianship. This set of factors—ongoing working relationships, knowledge of and commitment to information user-group goals and objectives, and highly customized and value-added contributions to the group—define embedded librarianship and set it apart from both traditional reference work and other initiatives to reach out and liberate the librarian from the library.

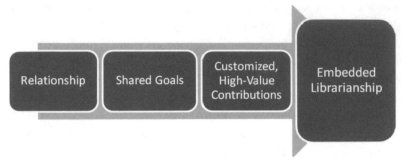

Figure 1.1 Factors That Define Embedded Librarianship

Embedded Librarians and Physical Location

The term *embedding* suggests a physical process. Embedded journalists live with military units, sharing in their experiences and observing their routines and combat actions in a theater of war. Some embedded librarians can be physically embedded. Michael Moore (2006) of the MITRE Corp. wrote that "things changed quickly" for him when his office moved into the area occupied by the group he was working with. Jill Stover Heinze (2010), of Affinion Loyalty Group, had a similar experience. When she moved into the Brand Communications group's space, she began participating in the informal conversations that sprang up as the group worked through its tasks—and they began to recognize the value of her contributions. Academic librarians such as Russell Hall (2008) spend time in the classroom, participating in discussions and teaching units on information literacy.

Such physical embedding of librarians, while common, is far from universal. Just as the modern environment of ubiquitous digital information means that people don't have to come to the library for the same reasons they used to, it also means the librarian can "get out of the library" without physically leaving the library. At one international law firm, for example, a librarian in the New York office is embedded with a major practice group of the firm. She does in-depth research, monitors hot topics, edits customized news, and stewards the group's shared document repository, along with its taxonomy. But she rarely sees the practice group leader face-to-face, because he works in the Los Angeles office. Other group members are scattered around the globe, so she rarely sees them, too (Shumaker and Talley, 2009, Appendix B).

In the academic sector, librarians at a number of institutions have embedded themselves virtually. At the Community College of Vermont, the library staff members have moved to an all-virtual embedding model, in which they participate in online courses and in the online course management system for face-to-face courses but never attend face-to-face classes (Matthew and Schroeder, 2006). Other institutions that have established virtual embedding include the University of Minnesota Extension and the Tennessee state college system (Mastel, 2011; York and Vance, 2009). To date, there is no evidence that virtual embedding is any less successful than an embedded relationship that involves physical colocation. While it can be easier to develop a strong working relationship face-to-face, experience indicates that it can also be done successfully via digital technologies.

Examples of Embedded Librarianship

Examples of embedded librarianship can be found in a variety of institutions and organizational sectors. Here are just a few to illustrate their diversity.

Johnson & Wales University

Johnson & Wales University in North Miami, Florida, specializes in preparing students for jobs in the hospitality industry, including hotel restaurants. Librarians Nicole Covone and Mia Lamm wrote about their role in *Public Services Quarterly* in 2010. They initiated their embedded role out of a realization that "the librarians on campus needed to cultivate a variety of relationships to successfully integrate library support into the curriculum" (p. 199). They viewed this initiative as a direct way to build trust, develop understanding of the librarians' role in learning, and become co-creators with the faculty.

Among other projects, they collaborated with faculty of the College of Culinary Arts to develop the research component of culinary assignments. One aspect of their collaboration was to deliver information literacy instruction to students in the classrooms—including kitchens. They wrote that these sessions were "often scheduled while the bread dough was rising and students were cleaning their workstations. As challenging as this teaching environment was, by entering their workspace we felt it moved us past the barrier of the reference desk. This one initiative enabled the librarian to step into nine baking and pastry lab classes resulting in outreach to approximately 10% of the student body. Students viewed the librarian as more approachable and understanding of the particular needs of culinary-focused students" (Covone and Lamm, 2010, p. 198).

Ziba Design

Reece Dano and Gretchen McNeely, librarians at Ziba Design in Portland, Oregon, tell this story, which comes from a presentation they gave at the 2010 Special Libraries Association (SLA) conference, a webinar they presented, and an interview published in the SLA magazine, *Information Outlook* (Dano and McNeely, 2010; Spencer, 2009).

Ziba Design is a small consulting firm with a couple of hundred employees. As consultants, employees take on projects related to diverse applications of design—everything from the branding and marketing initiatives of an athletic equipment manufacturer to assistance to an architect with the design of a transport station for the city of Portland.

Project teams are assembled dynamically to execute the various engagements. Typically, core team members are supplemented by others as needed. The librarians are frequently involved as either core members or supplementary members of the project teams. Initially, their role was to bring external, published, open source information to bear on the business problem confronting the group. However, the embedded librarians' role at Ziba grew beyond finding the published literature. They became more highly integrated into the engagement teams, contributing to primary research as well as providing the essential secondary research available from open sources.

Reece described an engagement that showcased the librarian's ability to transcend a traditional role and become the "information curator" for the team. The project's goal was to design a public transport station in a depressed community known as Rockwood. The design needed to be safe and welcoming as well as functional. It needed to take into consideration community input and be consistent with the nature and needs of the community. Reece began the process by conducting detailed research into the history and sociology of the community, using records from the local historical society, government census data, and other published sources. As a result, he became the most knowledgeable member of the team when it came to the character of the community, so he was chosen to guide the team on a visit to the area. As the team walked through the streets, observing the architecture and character of the neighborhood, one of the other members expressed the wish to talk to more members of the community. With his smartphone, Reece determined that they were a short distance from the local public library. He led the team to it, and once there, the team interviewed library users and the very knowledgeable library staff, gaining many new insights.

Reece went far beyond traditional library service in this situation. He didn't locate a set of references to source material and stop there. He didn't furnish copies of documents and stop there. He didn't write a report on the community and stop there. He did all these things and combined them with leading primary research into the community's needs. As he says, "I became ... both a docent and an information curator. In all, this approach made the entire research team more flexible, smarter and more efficient. The success of this approach led me to be used in a similar way in following projects" (Dano).

American University

Next, consider the work of Nobue Matsuoka-Motley at the American University in Washington, D.C. Nobue is the embedded music and performing arts librarian, with an office in the University's Katzen Center for the Performing Arts, at the opposite end of campus from the main university library. She's not just the embedded librarian; she is also a musician. She described her experiences in the *Public Services Quarterly* in 2010. In her case, it took extensive negotiations between the university librarian and the department of performing arts to acquire an office for her in the Performing Arts Center. Once she had it, she was able to leverage it to expand her relationships and her role with the faculty and students. Here are a few of her observations:

> It was crucial for me to become a community member to fully learn about [the faculty] and their needs. We serve a unique community where many things are accomplished through teamwork. The faculty and students constantly work together to accomplish their creative works. ... In such an environment everyone learns everyone else's name and strong bonds are developed.

Frequent opportunities to talk to the faculty made it easier to implement my initiatives to emphasize the importance of information literacy.

Since I became embedded in the [department of performing arts], the faculty has become accustomed to the concept of a librarian teaching information literacy to their students. During the first year after my move, the number of requests for in-class instruction increased 68% and item circulation jumped 21%. (Matos, Matsuoka-Motley, and Mayer, 2010, p. 130)

She concluded, "The success of embedded librarians depends upon the librarian's ability to understand the characteristics of the community they serve in addition to their ability and willingness to become a community member" (Matos, Matsuoka-Motley, and Mayer, 2010, p. 130).

University at Plattsburgh

Librarians Gordon Muir and Holly Heller-Ross (2010) have written about several embedded relationships they established at the State University of New York in Plattsburgh, New York. One of them is called the Biology Learning Community. The Biology 101 course syllabus sets forth this outcome for course learning: that students be able to pursue scholarly work, whether laboratory, field work, or literature synthesis, independently and as members of a team. The biology course is integrated with an 8-week library skills course that prepares students for the literature synthesis part of the assignment. The biology instructor and the librarian coordinated the two courses in advance. As they worked together, they realized that "the best time to assist students in their research is when the students are in lab and have questions, not when the students are out of lab and realize they need help and might not contact their librarian for research assistance" (p. 92). For this reason, the librarian became a full participant in the biology lab sessions.

Gordon and Holly draw several lessons from their experience. Here's one:

In order for librarians to be effective in the learning community, they must be viewed by all as a partner in the community. Real familiarity with the course and content (such as lab experiments) is vital to change the perception of students that the librarian is "just visiting" the lab and is not an integral part of the learning community. (Muir and Heller-Ross, 2010, p. 92)

Their overall advice for other academic librarians is as follows: "Time for planning and collaboration on assignments is essential for a successful partnership. Equally clear is the transformational nature of the new relationship. Once you are accepted as a member of the group of learners in the community, the barrier between the librarian and student is breached allowing for frequent and continual consultations to take place—both in the lab and outside of class, and throughout their academic career" (Muir and Heller-Ross, 2010, p. 92).

Affinion Loyalty Group

Jill Stover Heinze has spoken (Heinze and Kortash, 2009) and written (Heinze, 2010) about her experiences at the Affinion Loyalty Group, a unit of a larger corporation. Affinion specializes in marketing and advertising services for banking and other corporate clients. Heinze was hired as a research analyst to do competitive intelligence (CI), but she felt a bit disconnected until the company's president invited her to move her office into the Brand Communications group's area. Since then, Heinze has developed her role as an embedded librarian. Thanks to everyday informal interactions, members of the group began to realize what she could contribute, and she developed new insights into their work and goals. Now she finds herself contributing in ways both large and small. She is pulled into meetings to share her perspectives, contributes to corporate strategy, and serves as an expert in legislative and regulatory affairs that affect the company and its clients.

Heinze noted that her close collaboration with Brand Communications has yielded benefits all around:

> With each interaction between the CI librarian and the Brand professionals, knowledge is shared that ultimately influences the outputs of the Brand Communications group. The marketing materials developed today are far more advanced in terms of messaging and positioning than they were before the CI librarian was placed within the Brand group. Through this true partnership, each role gains greater understanding of our

> industry and how to position products, the company, and its
> clients to targeted audiences. (Heinze and Kortash, 2009, p. 10)

Heinze and her company have seen the value of embedded librarianship. She said, "partnering with someone with complementary skills can greatly improve each participant's own work while generating new opportunities to add value" (Heinze and Kortash, 2009, p. 10).

Each of these stories illustrates the key elements of embedded librarianship. There's a strong emphasis on relationships and the mutual understanding that comes with them. The librarian develops a thorough understanding of a university course or the work of a corporate business unit. Faculty and other professionals in turn come to appreciate the unique skills and perspectives that the librarian can add—skills and perspectives that become important factors in achieving desired outcomes. All of this results in the delivery of customized, high-value contributions to the work being done, and ultimately in shared responsibility for outcomes. Whether it's academic instruction or commercial research, these elements are consistent in all of the stories.

Advantages of Embedded Librarianship

The previous examples, and many others in the literature, illustrate five fundamental differences that enable the embedded librarian to achieve much more than traditional reference librarians can. Figure 1.2 illustrates these five differences.

Traditionally, librarians are responsive. As a matter of fact, we're known for our responsiveness. That's fine, but "responsive" implies waiting to be asked—an essentially passive model. Embedded librarians go a step further than responsiveness—they anticipate. A senior academic administrator I interviewed recently described the embedded librarian she works with as a "fount of ideas." A corporate administrator told me his embedded librarian suggested ways of accomplishing tasks that others on the team wouldn't think of—ways that save the team time and effort. Embedded librarians don't wait to be asked. They use their close working relationships to identify needs and find solutions.

The traditional model of library services is patrons getting help one at a time. The reality is that in government, the military, academia, and the corporate world, people work in teams. In educational settings, instructors are

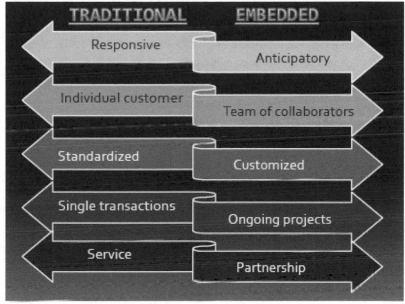

Figure 1.2 Differences Between Traditional and Embedded Librarianship

assigning team projects more and more often—to help students prepare for the collaborative world of work awaiting them. The embedded librarian, too, most often works with and for a team—a research group, a department, a student project team, or the students in a class. Embedded librarians are much more effective because they work for the whole team.

The traditional library service model is standardized and a bit bureaucratic. There are guidelines, policies, and standards of service. In some ways, those are all good things. The intent is to ensure equitable treatment to all. However, different teams have different needs, and what one team needs might not be so helpful to another. Flexibility becomes essential. The embedded librarian uses the strong working relationship formed through participation in a team to understand the team's needs and address them in a customized way.

Traditionally, transactions are the measure for reference work. With embedded librarianship, transactions still occur—documents are requested, instructional sessions are held, or documents are added to a shared virtual workspace—but the emphasis shifts from the transaction to the project. The counseling session with a student project team leads not just to questions, but also to discussions of options. The research project raises new questions that invite further research. The key news item spotted and distributed opens up a new task to track and report on changes. One action leads to another; one task flows into the next. The embedded librarian's work is evaluated by value added, by impact on student learning outcomes, or by team success, and not so much by the number of transactions completed.

Finally, the tradition of librarianship holds service as one of our highest values. The concept of service has many laudable connotations, and the profession of librarianship has a strong service ethic. Being service-oriented, treating people well, and caring about helping them effectively are good things. Yet, for all its positive associations, there are limits to service. The provider of a service stands a bit apart. The provider of a service is only responsible for that service. Embedded librarians are responsible for more than that.

You may note that I haven't used the term *service*, as in *library service* or *information service*, thus far in my explanations of embedded librarianship. That was a deliberate choice. Embedded librarians transcend service because they become partners. As a partner, the librarian is fully engaged. The partner is a member of a team whose members are mutually responsible for the overall outcome. It's different from the service relationship, and it's what happens when embedded relationships are fully developed.

Embedded Librarianship and Other Models of Librarianship

Thanks to a research grant from the SLA, I've spent more than 3 years studying embedded librarianship—trying to understand what it really is (and is not) and what factors make some librarians so successful at it. Along the way, I've found that the famous dictum "the future is already here, it's just unevenly distributed" (attributed to science fiction author William Gibson) applies well to the evolving model of embedded librarianship. Embedded librarianship is contending with the traditional model of reference work, along with other new models, as the profession develops strategies that will prove successful in that unevenly distributed future.

A broad consensus exists that the traditional model of reference services is fading away. It was never a very effective way to solve information problems anyway. There was a time when people had to rely on the library for information, but nowadays information is ubiquitous, and people have many sources from which to choose. For librarians, waiting at a reference desk for people to realize they need help and then get up the courage to ask for it may have been the best we could do at one time in history, but not anymore.

What should replace the traditional model? Librarians are trying different approaches, with titles such as *virtual librarian, roving librarian, personal librarian, consulting librarian,* and *embedded librarian.* Let's consider each one in turn.

The virtual librarian is available remotely via all kinds of communication media—phone, email, instant messaging, text messaging, and virtual worlds. The virtual librarian, thanks to schedule shifting and collaborative arrangements among librarians in different time zones and even different institutions, can also be available 24/7. But the virtual librarian is still in passive mode, waiting for people to come up to the virtual desk in cyberspace and ask a question.

The roving librarian "grows feet," to use one blogger's expression, and leaves the library to set up shop in different physical locations—a cafeteria, a student center, dorm lobbies and lounges, or different departments. Once there, the savvy librarian strikes up conversations with passersby, thereby encouraging them to ask questions that can open up new opportunities for librarians to assist with information needs. However, there are limits to this: If the librarian is scheduled to cover the cafeteria during lunchtime on Tuesday, she can't come to the new marketing project's kickoff meeting being held at the same time. What is really the better use of the librarian's time and attention? Furthermore, the librarian in the roving model is still disconnected from the work of the organization. Collaboration with faculty or business professionals is lacking. There's lots of energy in the roving librarian model, but it's not focused; it's diffused.

Some academic institutions are trying the personal librarian model. Entering first-year students are assigned a librarian to be their information counselor during their 4-year undergraduate career. The intent is to build relationships that enable the librarian to offer assistance proactively as well as encourage the student to reach out for assistance at critical junctures—when major term papers are assigned, for instance. Like the roving librarian, the personal librarian has opportunities to be proactive, but the possibility of a diffusion of energy is very real. The interests of first-year students aren't well defined and often shift during the student's undergraduate career. A personal librarian might have student clients majoring in music, physics, business, and nursing. It's impossible for any individual librarian to serve each of these areas equally well—our reputation for being outstanding generalists notwithstanding. The personal librarian approach also runs against the increasing emphasis on team projects: If you and I are on a team and we both have personal librarians, do we each go to our own librarian, or are we collaborating well enough that we decide together how our information needs will be handled? With the personal librarian model, it's left to chance, and the librarian isn't in a position to influence the approach. The personal librarian seeks relationships, but they are not founded on a clear purpose or focus.

Consulting librarians in any organizational setting—from a corporation to a university—combine mobility, proactivity, energy, and focus. Like any consultants, internal or external, they engage with a team or an individual client. They function as specialized role players with a unique expertise—in this case, information analysis and management—that the client needs in order to achieve certain objectives. They have the desirable attributes of "growing feet" and getting out of the library, both physically and virtually. They are proactive. They focus their energy on a team and are able to spot information problems that others on the team may not recognize. They are in a position to come up with solutions crafted to the special needs of the team. They establish relationships that last for the duration of the engagement and may continue beyond, into new engagements as well. (Every consultant, after all, has to keep an eye out for follow-on work and new tasks.) The consulting librarian model has much to recommend it and can dramatically expand the librarian's opportunities to deliver value to the organization. The only drawback is that consultants are typically viewed as specialized role players, not as full members of the team. The consultant contributes advice—sometimes solutions—but in a limited sphere bounded by preconceived ideas of the consultant's expertise. The consultant may not develop a strong knowledge of the team's work and may not feel a responsibility for overall team outcomes. Not viewed as a true member of the team, the consultant's advice is solicited only in situations in which the team members feel they need specialized expertise.

Finally, there's the embedded librarian. The embedded librarian contributes to a team or an organization through customized, specialized, high-value-added information management and analysis. Embedded librarianship, when fully developed, embraces a strong, ongoing working relationship between the librarian, team leaders, and other team members, and a sense of shared responsibility among all for outcomes and achievements. The embedded librarian develops a sophisticated under-standing of the team's domain. While the embedded librarian doesn't acquire the same level of expertise in a domain that other members have, the sophisticated understanding enables the librarian to become much more effective at customizing information solutions and adding value. The embedded librarian often contributes novel and useful insights and solutions to team problems that go beyond the expected bounds of the librarian's role. The embedded librarian combines proactivity and energy with strong working relationships, close alignment with team goals and objectives, shared responsibility for outcomes, and full membership in the team.

How Embedded Librarians Are Changing the Profession

Librarians bemoan the stereotypes that have dogged the profession for more than a century. Writing in the first volume of *American Library Journal*, Melvil Dewey alluded to the image of the librarian as a "mouser in musty books" (quoted in Bobrovitz and Griebel, 2001, p. 260) and called for the passing of that stereotype. A generation ago, there was hope that the dawn of information technology would "raise the phoenix of 'Marian the Librarian' from the ashes of mousiness"—a hope that was not fulfilled (Bobrovitz and Griebel, 2001, p. 260). Writing in 1000, Patricia Glass Schuman took the discussion of the professional stereotype to a new level:

> The image we seem to worry about most—that of the middle-aged spinster librarian—is basically irrelevant and unimpor-tant. What is important is the view of the librarian and the library as foreboding, boring, complicated, largely inaccessi-ble, or worse, irrelevant. (p. 86)

Schuman continues:

> Our focus should not be on how attractive people think we are (or even how smart) but how useful, necessary, and important we are to their education, research, and everyday lives and work. (p. 86)

This is exactly what embedded librarians are focusing on. They are finding ways to be important to the goals of the organizations in which they work. They are providing, in the words of Joan Durrance, "Well-focused services that require contact between a librarian and a client group within the context of a problem environment ... beyond answering the isolated reference question and into the role of a professional visibly helping the client solve problems" (quoted in Schuman, 1990, p. 86).

The embedded librarian is going even further than Durrance and Schuman advocated. The goal of embedded librarianship is more than service. It is partnership. The driving ideas behind it are that the effective use of information has become so critical to many social and business endeavors that librarians as information and knowledge experts can no longer stand apart from core organizational processes but must be fully engaged in them—not for the health of the profession, but for the health of the organizations and institutions in which they work. Where smart and enlightened executives are enabling motivated and effective librarians to step up to this new relationship, the old stereotypes of the retiring, irrelevant, clerical functionary arranging books on the shelves have disappeared in favor of the true image—a key player in the enterprise.

Summary

This chapter has begun our exploration of embedded librarianship by defining it and identifying the fundamental characteristics that set it apart from traditional library service practices.

Embedded librarianship is a distinct and different way for a librarian to work in any setting. The embedded librarian is fully integrated into a community. He or she forms strong working relationships with others, shares responsibility for the achievement of common goals, and makes a specialized contribution by applying advanced professional information competencies.

Five key characteristics that distinguish the embedded librarian from the traditional librarian are as follows:

- Embedded librarians aren't just responsive; they are able to anticipate information needs thanks to close communication and deep understanding of the work of the information user group.

- While the traditional librarian generally serves one library patron at a time, the embedded librarian typically interacts with an entire community of information users, and ensures that information flows to everyone in the group who needs it.

- The traditional library service model is standardized, but the embedded librarian customizes contributions to meet the most important needs of the user group. The librarian's strong working relationship with members of the group ensures that the customized information work is truly what the group needs most.

- Traditionally, transactions are the measure for reference work, but with embedded librarianship the emphasis shifts from the transaction to the project. One task flows into the next, and the embedded librarian is measured by value added, not transaction counts.

- In embedded librarianship the traditional value placed on service is superseded by the value of partnership, and shared ownership of team goals and objectives. Partnership emphasizes that the librarian is considered an integral member of the group, and not an adjunct role-player with limited participation.

This new model is replacing traditional reference librarianship, and is changing the profession at the same time—replacing outdated stereotypes with a new image of effective competence and engagement.

References

Bobrovitz, J., and R. Griebel. 2001. Still mousy after all these years: The image of the librarian in the 21st century. *Feliciter* 47 (5): 260–263.

Covone, N., and M. Lamm. 2010. Just be there: Campus, department, classroom ... and kitchen? *Public Services Quarterly* 6: 198–207.

Dano, R. Personal communication. November 16, 2010.

Dano, R., and G. McNeely. 2010. *Embedded librarianship in the field.* New Orleans, LA: Special Libraries Association.

Dene, J. 2011. Embedded librarianship at the Claremont Colleges. In *Embedded librarians: Moving beyond one-shot instruction*, eds. C. Kvenild and K. Calkins, 219–228. Chicago: Association of College and Research Libraries.

Hall, R. A. 2008. The "embedded" librarian in a freshman speech class: Information literacy instruction in action. *College & Research Libraries News* 69 (1): 28–30.

Heinze, J. S. 2010. Leveraging internal partnerships for library success. *Information Outlook* 14 (1): 13–15.

Heinze, J. S., and K. Kortash. 2009. Navigating through turbulent times: How the corporate special library and brand communications work together to forge a path to the future. Paper presented at Special Libraries Association annual conference, Washington, DC. Available from www.sla.org/pdfs/sla2009/navigating turbulenttimes_heinze.pdf. (Accessed April 4, 2012.)

Mastel, K. 2011. Extending our reach: Embedding library resources and services within extension. In *Embedded librarians: Moving beyond one-shot instruction,* eds. C. Kvenild and K. Calkins, 211–218. Chicago: Association of College and Research Libraries.

Matos, M. A., N. Matsuoka-Motley, and W. Mayer. 2010. The embedded librarian online or face-to-face: American University's experiences. *Public Services Quarterly* 6: 130–139.

Matthew, V., and A. Schroeder. 2006. The embedded librarian program: Faculty and librarians partner to embed personalized library assistance into online courses. *Educause Quarterly* 4: 61–65.

Moore, M. 2006. Embedded in systems engineering: How one organization makes it work. *Information Outlook* 10 (5): 23–25.

Muir, G., and H. Heller-Ross. 2010. Is embedded librarianship right for your institution? *Public Services Quarterly* 6: 92–109.

Schuman, P. G. 1990. The image of librarians: Substance or shadow. *Journal of Academic Librarianship* 16 (2): 86–89.

Shumaker, D., and M. Talley. 2009. *Models of embedded librarianship: Final report.* Alexandria, VA: Special Libraries Association.

Spencer, F. G. 2009. 10 questions: Reece Dano. *Information Outlook* 13 (3): 26–29.

York, A. C., and J. M. Vance. 2009. Taking library instruction into the online classroom: Best practices for embedded librarians. *Journal of Library Administration* 49 (1/2): 197–209.

Chapter 2

Push and Pull: The Forces Driving Embedded Librarianship

Embedded librarianship is growing. While there's no good way to analyze the trend quantitatively—there are no statistics on the number of "embedded librarians"—it seems clear from the literature that interest in alternatives to traditional library service is growing. For the past few years, there has been a steady stream of announcements of embedded librarianship programs on library websites. In 2010, *Public Services Quarterly* became the first professional journal to publish a special issue devoted to embedded librarianship. A year later, the Association of College and Research Libraries published the first professional book on the subject, *Embedded Librarianship: Moving Beyond One-Shot Instruction*.

What's driving this interest? Why are librarians seeking new models of library service, and what factors make embedded librarianship an attractive choice? This chapter explores the idea that a combination of "push" and "pull" factors is at work—the push of a widely recognized need for innovation in public services librarianship and the pull of fundamental changes in work and society. Figure 2.1 depicts these forces.

The push to innovate comes from the clear fact that the traditional model of reference services no longer works—which reflects how technological and social changes have changed how people use information. The pull to the embedded model derives from major trends that emphasize the importance of the knowledge worker; the challenge for the knowledge worker and the enterprise to be creative and to innovate as well as to be logical and exact; the imperative to develop and maintain a competitive advantage in the global economy; the need to measure and evaluate knowledge work; and perhaps most directly, the advantage of diverse teams and especially of cognitive diversity in achieving the other goals. This chapter will examine each of these factors in turn.

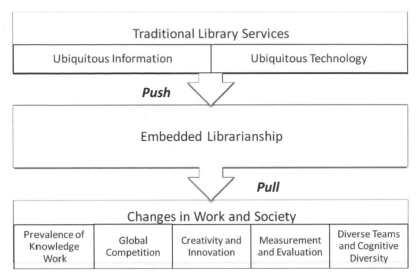

Figure 2.1   The Push and Pull of Embedded Librarianship

Push: Traditional Services That No Longer Work

For most of history, people thought of librarians primarily as the keepers of the books. The idea that librarians would deliberately try to help individuals seeking to use the books was a revolution that occurred less than 150 years ago. When, in 1876, Samuel Swett Green published his famous article, "Personal Relations Between Librarians and Readers," his ideal was the omniscient reference librarian, who could direct the reader to the proper source on any topic. The dominant metaphor was that of the retail establishment. As Green stated, "A librarian should be as unwilling to allow an inquirer to leave the library with his question unanswered as a shop-keeper is to have a customer go out of his store without making a purchase" (p. 74).

Our notions of library services advanced very little beyond Green's for more than 100 years. For generations, reference librarians sat passively at their reference desks, awaiting the next inquiry on "specimens of decorative painting" or "the ceremony of the Marriage of the Adriatic" (to cite two of Green's examples). However, in the past several decades, two things happened that make this approach problematic.

First, the profession has learned a lot about how people really interact with information. People don't always recognize an information need. Taylor (1968) has given us the concept of the *visceral information need—*

one that is not consciously recognized, not articulated, and not actively addressed. Information seekers often have difficulty in articulating their need: It may be felt, recognized, and even addressed, but the seeker may formulate it imprecisely. From this understanding, librarians have developed an emphasis on the reference interview—a valuable skill by which librarians gently elicit true needs from information seekers and aid them in finding the information they need. Finally, we have learned about the sources people turn to when they need information. They turn to their friends, their colleagues, their family, their officemates, or their classmates. They do not start with the library—or the reference librarian. Tenopir and King (2004), in their masterful review book, *Communication Patterns of Engineers*, have marshaled an imposing array of research to demonstrate that even highly educated technical professionals behave this way.

Armed with these new insights, Samuel Green's image of the omniscient reference librarian calmly disposing of miscellaneous queries from all comers, like a World Cup goalkeeper deflecting shots from a primary school forward or a major league baseball hitter calmly swatting a little leaguer's pitches out of the park, assumes an air of unreality. Childers (1980) notes that even in the 1960s and 1970s, Childers, Crowley, and others called into question the accuracy and completeness of responses given by reference librarians. We have learned that real-world information finding is much messier than Green's ideal. People don't stride into the library with fully formed, neatly articulated reference questions. When they ask something complex, a librarian requires context, domain knowledge, and especially feedback and iteration to get the answer right.

The second thing that happened to upset our 19th-century model of library service is the ubiquity of information. The era of information scarcity transformed into the era of information abundance. Enabled by the rise of information technologies—computers, communications systems, and the web—information has engulfed us. Adding to what we have learned about human information seeking (as synthesized by Tenopir and King, 2004), the Online Computer Library Center's *Perceptions of Libraries* (De Rosa, 2005) has established that the general public usually starts its searching on the web.

The effect on library reference services has been fundamental and, in some cases, cataclysmic. While people continue to visit libraries, they use them in very different ways from those envisioned by Green and the older generation of library service experts. American public libraries have experienced a noted increase in attendance in the past several years, but the primary purposes of visitors are to use computers, meet and work with friends, and find books to take out—not to ask reference questions. Similarly, academic library after academic library is moving print collections to compact storage or offsite—or disposing of the lesser-used parts of it. Librarians are reconfiguring space to align with the reasons students visit: to find a respite from the dormitory, a quiet place for individual study, or a rendezvous for group study (and socializing).

Two observations, one unsystematic and the other systematic, illustrate this point.

I teach a course titled Information Sources and Services, a core, required course that introduces students to the principles and practice of public services in libraries and information centers. The first course assignment I give is a field study. Students make an appointment to visit a library or information center of their choosing. They observe the activity in the library, shadow a reference librarian, and talk with the librarian about the nature of the work. The students who visit general public and academic libraries report experiences that belie the traditional notions of what goes on at the reference desk. By their observation and the reports of the librarians they interview, my students discover that almost all the transactions at the reference desk are directional ("Where's the bathroom?") or related to technology support ("Can you add paper to the printer?") or administration ("Can I get a password for the wireless network?"). Generally, they find that there's little substantive engagement with library users' information needs, even at the level advocated by Samuel Green.

More systematically, the revolution in access to digital information has had a catastrophic effect on traditional library reference services. The statistics reported by the members of the Association of Research Libraries (ARL) reveal the extent of this catastrophe. ARL is an organization of more than 100 large libraries, predominantly academic, in North America. It collects and publishes annual statistics of its membership, including statistics on reference transactions. From the 1999–2000 academic year to the 2008–2009 academic year, the number of reference transactions reported by ARL members fell by 45 percent, from more than 18.5 million to less than 10.3 million. The number of reporting institutions remained nearly constant during that period, and the mean number of transactions per institution fell by 46 percent, from more than 163,000 to less than 88,000. Figure 2.2 graphs the ARL data.

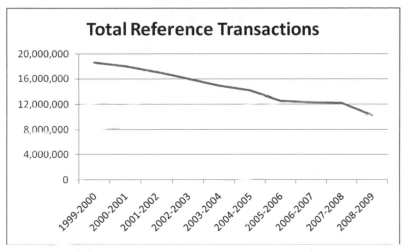

*Figure 2.2   Association of Research Libraries Member-Reported Reference
Transactions, 1999–2000 to 2008–2009. [Data from
www.arl.org/stats/annualsurveys/arlstats/statxls.shtml
(accessed July 5, 2011)]*

This change in behavior demonstrates that people no longer need to
visit a library to obtain most types of information. They are surrounded by
media. They have access to web search engines and web content from
their mobile devices. Libraries of all types are doing an increasingly effective job of replacing their print collections with remotely accessible web-
based digital collections. Information is abundant and ubiquitous. There
is an air of end-user self-sufficiency as well, justified or not, and people no
longer feel much need to visit the library for information or ask a librarian
for help.

Probably, the phenomenon of human information-seeking behavior
was never as simple as Samuel Green described it in 1876. The library reference desk is actually a very limited forum for resolving information
needs. Information technology has only exacerbated its limits. Thus, the
profession of librarianship is being pushed by these trends to find innovative ways to contribute to resolving people's information-related problems in society and organizations of all types. As Dakshinamurti and
Satpathy (2009) suggested, "The fact that technology allows the users to
have direct access to the products of information has paradoxically made
it all the more necessary for the librarian to reach out to the users in a
proactive manner" (p. 1).

Pull: Fundamental Trends in Work and Society

The spread of abundant, ubiquitous information has magnified the flaws in the 19th-century model of library services and set librarians on a search for new models. At the same time, the following trends in work and society are opening up new opportunities, which embedded librarians are uniquely positioned to exploit:

- The importance of knowledge work and the knowledge worker
- The imperative to develop and maintain a competitive advantage in the global economy
- The importance of creativity and innovation
- The need to measure and evaluate knowledge work
- The advantage of diverse teams and especially of cognitive diversity

The Importance of Knowledge Work and the Knowledge Worker

Developed economies and societies are dominated by knowledge work and knowledge workers. In these societies, knowledge is being created at an ever-increasing pace, and innovative tools and methods are constantly replacing old ones. Educators have recognized that whatever body of knowledge they impart today will be superseded tomorrow. To sustain themselves for a lifetime as knowledge workers, members of society must learn how to learn. They must be lifelong learners. In other words, they must become and remain information literate. Accordingly, information literacy—which includes the ability to recognize information needs, to evaluate and use information effectively, and to use finding skills—has been widely recognized as a core educational outcome at all levels.

The fact that we are living in the Age of Information also means that institutions of all types—businesses, nonprofits, and governmental bodies—recognize that their organizational performance is dependent on their ability to use information and share knowledge effectively. In every organization, success depends on "knowing what we know" internally, as well as effectively identifying and using the world's knowledge.

In this context of increasing emphasis on personal information literacy and corporate knowledge management, librarians are the sole professional group with a tradition of concern for the need, pursuit, management, retrieval, and use of information and knowledge. The trends of this age ought to be, and indeed are, ready-made opportunities for librarians to step in and make important contributions.

In primary, secondary, and higher education, librarians are the members of the academic community who have the skills of information literacy as their professional focus. Accordingly, they've become information literacy instructors. In many cases they function as guest lecturers, brought into class sessions or having classes brought to them in their libraries, for single (so-called one-shot) presentations on literature search and library use skills. In other settings, though, their engagement has been deeper and more enduring. Professionals in higher education recognize the importance of putting information literacy instruction in context. Academics appreciate the importance of relating it to real course work and student interests and of providing the range of conceptual introduction, hands-on practice, review and reflection, and evaluation. In the institutions that take this approach, librarians give presentations, develop instructional modules, help shape research assignments, grade them, and counsel student project teams. What's more, they sit as full partners in curriculum review and development committees, where they contribute their insights on information literacy, as well as other matters. These are the librarians who are embedded in the instructional mission.

Similarly, in business enterprises, nonprofit organizations, medical facilities, and governmental units, librarians are the sole professional group that concentrates on providing the technical and business information needed to further the organization's mission. While traditionally their primary focus was delivering external information in the form of books, serials, technical reports, and the like, they often played an informal knowledge management role. They developed an overview of the information needs, and therefore the interests and expertise, of professionals in different units of the enterprise. They could use their insights to link individuals with common interests or to suggest who might have expertise relevant to a particular question or problem. Still, the ability of the librarian to play a key role and add value by facilitating the effective sharing of knowledge is sometimes limited by a variety of factors. Not least among them is the librarian's location in a library, often set apart from the office areas of the library users, and the librarian's focus on the stewardship of the library collection.

Where enlightened corporate leaders and library leaders see the potential and free librarians from these constraints, librarians become embedded

in work groups and prove themselves able to deliver value through facilitating the effective sharing and use of information and knowledge—and
in other ways. This development is very much in line with recommendations made by Davenport and Prusak in 1993:

> It is time for a new model of the corporate library and the librar-
> ian. The warehouse concept must be blown up: librarians, or
> rather information managers, must view themselves not as
> warehouse custodians, or even as providers of centralized
> expertise, but rather as overseers of a multi-media network. …
> Broadly speaking, the role of the information professional
> becomes the establishment of connections between those who
> have information, and those who want it. (p. 408)

Davenport (1997) in his book, *Information Ecology*, revisited this point:

> The ideal information staff not only passively accepts user
> requests but also actively develops information sources, chan-
> nels, and programs for users who don't yet know they need the
> information. In a sense, ecological information professionals
> become evangelists, constantly attempting to recruit new
> members and provide new services to those members, even
> before they ask. They are familiar—but not obsessed—with key
> information technologies. Most important, such providers are
> highly responsive when users do ask for information, and
> understand its business context. In other words, their *raison
> d'être* is adding value to information. (p. 116)

Clearly, the prevalence of knowledge work in modern society offers an
opportunity to librarians willing to seize it.

The Imperative to Develop and Maintain a Competitive Advantage in the Global Economy

Outsourcing and its international cousin offshoring are now a fact of economic life. Starting with basic manufacturing and relatively low-skilled
professions, the shift of business functions and jobs from nations with
high labor costs to nations with lower labor costs permeates almost every
industry and profession. Call centers, software development, and

accounting work have all been subject to this trend. Even surgical proce-
dures have been "offshored," through so-called medical tourism, in which
patients travel abroad to undergo surgery at prices dramatically lower
than those in effect at home.

Library services have also been subject to this trend. In the U.S., contract providers of reference, document delivery, and other services have
become well established. In the age of digital collections, the same functions can be, and have been, performed outside the country for U.S.
clients. For librarians, as for other professionals affected by offshore competition, there are two options. First, reduce costs in order to compete on
price with the offshore providers. Second, either establish a competitive
position that adds value to justify the higher cost or otherwise occupy a
role that is simply impractical to outsource.

For a number of years, author Thomas Friedman has studied the
nature of global economic competition and job migration. In his book *The
World Is Flat* (2005), Friedman advocated that everyone should strive to
become an "untouchable." "Untouchables," he explained, "are people
whose jobs cannot be outsourced" (p. 238). He identified four categories
of untouchables: workers who are special, workers who are specialized,
those who are "anchored," and those who are exceptionally adaptable.

Embedded librarians have attributes of two of these categories: specialization and adaptability, and possibly a third, anchoring. Very, very few
librarians can claim to be "special" in Friedman's terms. In this category
belong the sports superstars, popular entertainment icons, and mega-
entrepreneurs whose names are household words.

On the other hand, embedded librarians are specialized, or at least
become specialized over time. While many do not have specialized knowledge when they begin an embedded engagement, almost all develop a
substantial understanding of the work of their teams over time (Shumaker
and Talley, 2009). Whether they work with engineers, marketers, medical
doctors, or other professionals, they must develop an understanding of
their partners' domain that allows them to recognize information needs,
grasp how information will be used, and act intelligently to fill information gaps. The embedded librarian who requires a basic explanation of the
context every time a sophisticated information problem arises is not des-
tined to remain in the role. This stands in sharp contrast to the orientation
of traditional library services as articulated by Green and practiced by
generations of librarians ever since. The traditional reference librarian
isn't assumed to have any particular background knowledge, but to be a

generalist able to address any and all questions equally. This has always been a myth, of course, but it invites the perception of librarians as lacking the contextual knowledge to handle challenging questions. Embedded librarianship destroys this perception. Embedded librarians are valued and trusted for their ability to combine their specialized context knowledge and knowledge of specialized information sources and processing methods with their generalized information management competencies in a way that adds unique value.

Successful embedded librarians are also adaptable. Adaptability means identifying new ways to add value and learning new skills in order to stay at the forefront as tools and methods advance. Friedman (2005) told the story of his friend Bill Greer, a freelance graphic artist. Greer's traditional services were displaced by the advent of computerized graphic design in the late 1990s, so he learned the new tools. But that added skill only kept him even, competitively, with many other designers who could use the same tools. So Greer adapted further. He began to use his creative gifts to specialize in coming up with overall concepts and quick sketches that would communicate effectively and could be turned into finished artwork by others lower in the value chain. Yet another effect of technological change caused Greer to adapt even further. He found a need for expertise in *morphing*: reshaping images, such as faces, so that one image turns into another over a series of panels. He adapted by becoming an expert in this new field, which opened up a line of business for himself that had not previously existed.

Embedded librarians are like Bill Greer. As basic information becomes ubiquitous and other professionals are able to obtain for themselves some types of information they formerly would have had to ask a librarian for, embedded librarians are able to adapt. They become the early adopters of new tools. They can help their colleagues become even more self-sufficient while also applying their unique blend of domain knowledge and information management knowledge to do more-sophisticated information retrieval, analysis, and synthesis tasks. The nature of embedded librarians' tasks varies. Some primarily do research and analysis, some teach or co-teach, some steward information and knowledge for their teams. The common thread is that all deliver some form of highly valued, sophisticated contributions, not simply basic reference, document delivery, or similar functions. They have adapted to move beyond the traditional library services.

Embedded librarians also have a degree of anchoring. *Anchoring,* according to Friedman (2005), refers to jobs that simply must be done in a certain location. Getting a haircut or having your office cleaned simply can't be done offshore, so barbers and custodians are "anchored." Certain forms of traditional librarianship are also anchored: The public library children's librarian is unlikely to be offshored anytime soon; it's hard to imagine the librarian's storytime being replaced by a video monitor with a story being read (probably recorded, and not live) by someone 10 or 12 time zones away. However, other forms of traditional librarianship are susceptible to offshoring. Straightforward literature searching and reference work are examples; basic web coding is another. These are transactional activities. Embedded librarians operate at a level at which their relationships with other members of their organizations are essential. These relationships don't always depend on physical proximity, but in many cases they are aided by informal and social interactions that do result from physical colocation. These interactions provide critical context and understanding that allow the embedded librarian to be a highly valued contributor to the team.

The Importance of Creativity and Innovation

Daniel Pink (2006) echoed much of Friedman's argument, using recent advances in the understanding of brain physiology as his framework. He made the distinction between the rational processes governed by the left hemisphere of the brain (what he calls *L-Directed* work) and the creative and innovative capabilities that reside in the brain's right hemisphere (which he terms *R-Directed*). In his book *A Whole New Mind,* he asserted that "[i]f standardized, routine L-Directed work such as many kinds of financial analysis, radiology, and computer programming can be done for a lot less overseas and delivered to clients instantly via fiber optic links, that's where the work will go" (p. 39). As a result, he continued, "many of today's knowledge workers will likewise have to command a new set of aptitudes. They'll need to do what workers abroad cannot do equally well for much less money—using R-Directed abilities such as forging relationships rather than executing transactions, tackling novel challenges instead of solving routine problems, and synthesizing the big picture rather than analyzing a single component" (pp. 39–40). That's a pretty good description of the role that successful embedded librarians, such as the ones introduced in Chapter 1, play in their organizations.

Just as adaptability is an essential attribute for individuals in the age of global competition, it is also essential for the enterprise. The organization that fails to keep up with changing needs and changing methods of operation will find itself increasingly marginalized and ultimately irrelevant. This is equally true in the for-profit sector and with nonprofits such as institutions of higher education. In fact, the lines between for-profit and nonprofit are blurring in some fields, as for-profit educational enterprises, for example, aggressively expand the use of distance education and appeal to new demographic groups, revolutionizing the field formerly dominated by traditional colleges and universities. Meanwhile, sheer budget pressure forces government bodies at all levels to reexamine their operations and do more with less.

Managers, and scholars of management, have learned that the industrial-age model of scientific management is not the way to engender the required organizational flexibility and adaptability. Pink (2006) highlighted this point in a variety of illustrations of successful organizations that are deploying R-Directed capabilities and contributors to augment their traditional L-Directed strengths. He mentioned examples such as management consultants McKinsey & Co., which reduced the proportion of MBA degree holders in its ranks from a majority to a minority during a 10-year period (p. 54), and the World Bank, which adopted a story-based approach to knowledge management (storytelling being an R-Directed activity) as a strategy to improve its organizational performance (pp. 105–106).

The dichotomy between left brain rational thinking and analysis, on one hand, and right brain creativity and innovation, as reflected in storytelling, pattern recognition, and synthesis, on the other, captures the difference between traditional librarianship and the embedded model.

As detailed in Chapter 1, traditional library services are transactional in concept, and the librarian focuses on providing a specific response to a specific question. The recent trend is that most reference questions tend toward the most basic—simple directional and bibliographic queries. Yet a countercurrent noted by some reference librarians—that at the high end, more-sophisticated questions are being asked—should be a sign of the latent demand for embedded librarians. Meanwhile, the traditional librarian, lacking strong working relationships, neither knows the stories nor sees the big picture and thus lacks opportunities to contribute much of a right brain, creative, synthesized nature.

The embedded librarian, by contrast, establishes strong working relationships, knows the stories, and is sometimes the team member best able to tell them. The embedded librarian is often a bit of an outlier—someone whose skills and perspectives are more different than those of others. Not only does this uniqueness enable the librarian to spot unrecognized information needs; it also puts the librarian into the position of suggesting creative solutions and approaches that others might not identify.

Finally, it has been noted that creative solutions sometimes arise from the juxtaposition of two seemingly unrelated phenomena. Peter Drucker (Drucker and Maciariello, 2004) noted several examples of this phenomenon: The zipper was invented for closing bales of heavy goods, not for use on clothing, and clothing manufacturers resisted its introduction because they viewed it as being inferior to buttons. Fiberglass cables, which have revolutionized telecommunications, were invented not by telecommunications companies, but by a glass company, Corning. As Drucker (1998) also noted, external knowledge is one of senior management's most pressing needs: "We can already discern and define the next, and perhaps even more important, task in developing an effective information system for top management: the collection and organization of OUTSIDE-focused information" (p. 52). The librarian's professional focus on information—information from diverse sources—becomes an asset in this context. The librarian should be the team member who introduces diverse elements to contribute to innovative, creative problem solving. Pink (2006) called this *symphony*: "the ability to put together the pieces ... to synthesize rather than analyze; to see relationships between seemingly unrelated fields; to detect broad patterns rather than to deliver specific answers; and to invent something new by combining elements nobody else thought to pair" (p. 126).

As organizations of all types increasingly recognize the necessity of integrating left brain analytics with right brain symphony, librarians have an important role to play and exciting opportunities to pursue. Unfortunately, traditional library service modes inhibit them. Embedded librarianship frees them to take advantage of these opportunities.

The Need to Measure and Evaluate Knowledge Work

Pink (2006) took care to point out that right brain creative skills do not replace left brain analytical abilities. As he said, "L-Directed Thinking remains indispensable. It's just no longer sufficient" (p. 51). One manifestation of the continuing importance of rigorous analytical thinking is the increasing emphasis on evaluation in almost every realm of economic life.

Indeed, left brain thinking, in the form of an emphasis on measurement and evaluation, is yet another force pulling librarians in the direction of embedded librarianship.

As developed by Frederick W. Taylor and others, objective, "scientific" management was a great step forward in management of industrial organizations during the period from the late 19th to the late 20th century. In librarianship, one expression of scientific management was a mania for counting—counting the size of collections, the number of volumes added, the number of interlibrary loans, the number of reference questions asked, and so on and on. The passion for counting continues to this day. It does have its value. After all, statistics from the ARL helped portray the decline of traditional reference services.

The important question, though, is what to measure. Traditional library evaluations have focused on inputs, activities, and outputs (we bought so many books, we cataloged so many books, and we circulated so many books). Sometimes statistics gathered on user satisfaction, as in the ARL's LibQual+ surveys, contribute to library evaluations. Meanwhile, corporations have concentrated on measuring value. Peter Drucker (1998) traced this focus to the rise of activity-based accounting in the 1980s. He noted that activity-based accounting "is not designed to *minimize* costs. It is designed to *maximize* yields. It focuses on the creation of value rather than the avoidance of waste" (p. 50; italics in the original). In other words, modern business evaluation focuses on the value added by each activity and each process.

The focus on measuring value added spread to primary and secondary education because of concerns about the quality of student learning. It took the form of demands for *accountability*—evidence that the educational processes and methods being practiced actually resulted in student achievement, or mastery of important knowledge and skills. Ultimately, it infiltrated American higher education as well. As postsecondary education becomes increasingly competitive, colleges and universities adopt institutional and course-specific learning outcomes. They insist that instructors tie student evaluations (i.e., grades) to the measurement of those learning outcomes.

While financial measures of value remain important, the drive for evaluation and measurement of outcomes has gone further, into qualitative as well as quantitative outcomes. Drucker (1999) recognized that in the world of knowledge work, quality is central:

> In most knowledge work, quality is not a minimum and a restraint. Quality is the essence of the output. In judging the performance of a teacher, we do not ask how many students there can be in his or her class. We ask how many students learn anything—and that's a quality question. (p. 84)

Against this backdrop, the traditional library preoccupation with measuring inputs, activities, and outputs, and sometimes user satisfaction, is not good enough. Libraries, like other organizational units, are being held accountable for their contribution to organizational outcomes—whether those outcomes are financial or learning-related or the achievement of corporate missions. Whatever the corporate strategy, libraries and librarians must demonstrate their contributions, in terms understood and valued by the managers of the institution.

The greatest obstacle for librarians who seek to demonstrate their value is that the library as a unit stands apart from the work of the institution. If an engineer gains a critical insight as a result of reading a technical article in a library-provided online database, is the librarian ever likely to hear about it? Possibly, but as a rule there is no systematic way for this to happen. If student research improves as a result of the library's information literacy instruction modules, is there a way to trace the effect back to the cause? Again, the system provides no mechanism for that to occur.

Embedded librarianship is different. One of the joys commonly expressed by embedded librarians is that they experience firsthand the impact of their work. They know how they are affecting outcomes, because they are in constant communication with the other staff members who are working toward the same goals they are. What's more, the information users, and their managers, also directly see the extent of the librarian's impact. In the academic setting, it is common for research projects to be graded partially on the quality of information sources used and the effectiveness with which they are used. The embedded librarians are sometimes the ones doing the grading. In this way, information literacy outcomes relate back directly to information literacy instruction, provided by the embedded librarian. As Shumaker and Talley (2009) noted about their interview with one such instructor:

> The Associate Professor of Biology reports that she can see the differences among sophomores between those who took the Great Problems course as first-year students (and had contact

with the librarians) and those who didn't. The information literacy skills developed in the Great Problems course stay with the
students and enable them to perform better. (Appendix B, p. 13)

Rigorous evaluation may be quantitative or qualitative. It may consist of
numerical scores, achievement of targets for profits or sales, or testimonials and anecdotes. The nature of the evaluation is driven by the nature of
the work and the culture of the organization. The common threads are that
the assessment of value is a fact of life in almost all organizations, and that
the embedded librarian is in a much stronger position to demonstrate
value than is the traditional practitioner of library services.

The Advantage of Diverse Teams and Cognitive Diversity

No matter what type of organization you work in, it probably uses teams
to accomplish many different tasks. Teamwork and knowledge work go
hand in hand. As Davenport (1997) said, "A participative approach to
information and knowledge work processes that emphasizes outcome,
not detailed work steps—along with external factors such as common
physical location and working in teams—will probably deliver the best
results" (p. 155).

In educational settings, instructors are encouraged to use team assignments in order to give students experience for the team-oriented world
they'll encounter when they enter the labor force. In higher education,
faculty committees have been a fixture for generations, but in some
enlightened institutions, they have evolved into multidisciplinary teams
that address curriculum development, distance learning, and other key
initiatives. In the business world, leaders have recognized that getting
research and development, production, marketing, and sales staff
together in product development teams greatly increases the chance of
success when the product launches in the marketplace. Even in large academic and public library systems, library directors form crossfunctional
teams of catalogers, systems librarians, and reference librarians to accomplish major initiatives, rather than leaving the task in the hands of a single
group of specialists.

As Jon Katzenbach and Douglas Smith (1993) put it in their classic book
The Wisdom of Teams, "Teams outperform individuals acting alone or in
larger organizational groupings, especially when performance requires
multiple skills, judgments, and experiences" (p. 9). The prevalence of

crossfunctional teams in organizational life is the fifth force pulling librarians to adopt the embedded model. After all, when all the other professionals in an organization are accomplishing essential work in teams, librarians can ill afford to stand apart. Librarians must embed themselves in these teams and make unique contributions that directly affect the quality of the projects.

Embedded librarians make two kinds of contributions to the teams with which they are embedded. The first is the obvious one. They contribute information delivery and information management so that the quality of information used by the team is improved. Better information leads to better outcomes, sometimes in marginal ways and sometimes in dramatic ways. The second kind of contribution may not be so obvious. Embedded librarians are a source of cognitive diversity that increases the pool of understanding and solutions within the team as it goes about its work—and this too has been shown to be a contributing factor to team performance—sometimes in dramatic ways.

The human information-seeking behavior discussed earlier in this chapter is reinforced in teams. People tend to start looking for information with the sources closest to them: their friends, their officemates, their colleagues on a team, and the web. Team problems tend to be addressed inside the team. The team can pull in outside resources, such as librarians, as needed for help with specific questions. But doing that is a last resort. Most problems are addressed within the team, by core team members. This means that many information needs never get to the library; questions never get asked at the reference desk. The embedded librarian, by being present and participating in team meetings, can identify the unasked question and can address it right away. (The embedded librarian can address the asked question, too!) "Addressing the question" may take the form of identifying and providing published information or other external information. It may also take the form of internal knowledge management—helping the team find and engage experts within the organization. Whether the sources are internal or external, the embedded librarian is well-positioned to deliver the best information to the team at the right time, in the right way.

Teams have other information problems that embedded librarians are uniquely able to solve. Many teams generate information. Briefings, position papers, working documents, drafts, and informal communications are artifacts of the team's process and progress. Many teams recognize the need to capture and refer to these artifacts. They use tools to help them—

an open source wiki in one case, a sophisticated commercial application such as SharePoint in another.

Team members sometimes think adopting one of these enterprise search tools will take care of the problem. If the project is a complex one, they soon learn otherwise. As the volume of documentation grows, the lack of an organizing principle to match becomes evident, and the complaint arises, "I know the documents are in here, but I can't find anything anymore." At this point, the team may turn to a librarian–knowledge manager, who can create a taxonomy, help categorize the documents, and provide stewardship of the system to overcome the problem of findability. The embedded librarian, of course, is perfectly positioned to prevent this problem in the first place, by setting up systems and processes that will grow as the team develops its project. Because embedded librarians understand the mission and goals, the domain and the terminology, and the major challenges faced by the team, they can apply information management skills most effectively for the team.

The first contribution of embedded librarians to teams is obvious: the effective application of information skills to the work of the team. The second is more subtle: the addition of relevant cognitive diversity to the team. Put another way, librarians think differently, and that can be a very good thing for a team. Katzenbach and Smith (1993) pointed out that one reason teams are effective is that "they bring together complementary skills and experiences that, by definition, exceed those of any individual on the team" (p. 18).

In his book *The Difference* (2007), Scott Page, a professor at the University of Michigan, made the case for what he calls "the Diversity Conjecture: Diversity leads to better outcomes" (p. 4). Page's argument is that teams made up of cognitively diverse people perform better than do individual experts or teams made up of members who all have the same background, same education, and same ways of thinking. (As Page expressed it, "diversity trumps ability" and "diversity trumps homogeneity" [p. 10].) There are conditions: He also noted that the diverse cognitive skills must be relevant to the nature of the problem at hand.

The application to embedded librarianship is this: Librarians possess unique perspectives; interpretations; heuristics, or approaches to problem solving; and models of cause and effect. They develop these cognitive tools from their education and experience in the field of information and knowledge management. When embedded into teams where their unique cognitive tools are appropriate, they can make an irreplaceable contribution to the work of the team.

Embedded librarians in higher education provide a simple example of this. Every experienced academic reference librarian can tell stories of helping students cope with ill-conceived research projects. A faculty member who doesn't really understand information retrieval nor have a good grasp of information literacy skills devises an assignment intended to get students into the library and expose them to scholarly information resources. Alas, the project is unrealistic, and the librarian is left holding the bag: helping the student figure out a way to satisfy the requirements of the assignment without going berserk in the process. Smart reference librarians find their way back to the instructor, to discuss the nature of the assignment and suggest improvements for next term.

When the librarian is embedded into the department's instructional strategy, these information train wrecks don't happen. Faculty members consult the librarian in advance when developing research-related assignments. The librarian collaborates, articulating the information literacy objectives to be achieved, shaping the assignment to the information skills of the students, the objectives, and the tools and resources available. The librarian serves as the students' information guide–consultant–instructor through the project process, and in some cases, the librarian also takes responsibility for grading the information literacy component of the product. The embedded librarian, in short, contributes to a better outcome for all by applying a special set of cognitive skills.

Katzenbach and Smith (1993) added one more factor to the reasons diverse teams outperform: motivation, or shared commitment to objectives. They said, "Teams are more productive than groups that have no clear performance objectives because their members are committed to deliver tangible performance results" (p. 15). The librarian who becomes embedded in the team not only understands team objectives but also commits to them. The librarian becomes a trusted partner on the team, not a service provider who stands apart but a partner fully integrated into the team. This relationship is integral to the concept of embedded librarianship.

Summary

This chapter has explored the forces pushing and pulling librarians toward the embedded model. We have seen that the traditional library service model, which served the profession well for more than a century, no longer fits with changes in information technology and society as a whole. People simply use information differently now. The misalignment in the library service model is reflected in measures of traditional library service, such as the ARL's reference statistics. The decline of the old model is pushing innovative librarians to find new ways to deploy their expertise.

On the "pull" side, I summarized key trends that open up new opportunities for embedded librarians:

- The primacy of knowledge work in developed economies of the 21st century puts a premium on information and knowledge and the skills to use them: the forte of the embedded librarian.

- The globalization of economic competition demands adaptation, specialization, and relationship building on the part of individuals and organizations.

- Technical skills and rational thought processes are no longer sufficient; embedded librarians open up opportunities to apply both right brain and left brain aptitudes.

- Everyone, and every professional specialty, is accountable in modern organizations; successful embedded librarians are visible, and their contributions are recognized by managers and others.

- The dominant form of corporate behavior is teamwork. Embedded librarians do not stand apart; they place themselves into teams as "integral parts to the whole."

The reader may think that all of these theories sound good, but wants to ask one further question: Does it work? Is there evidence that embedded librarianship really delivers the goods, both for the organization and for the librarian? The answer is this: Embedded librarianship can work—but it is not guaranteed. There are principles and practices that contribute to success, and there are many examples of success in a variety of organizations. In the next chapters, I'll review the trends and discuss the examples of success in a wide range of settings. Then I'll turn to principles of successful embedded librarianship and how to develop a customized roadmap to success for your organization.

References

Childers, T. 1980. The test of reference. *Library Journal* 105 (8): 924–928.

Dakshinamurti, G. B., and K. C. Satpathy. 2009. The pro-active academic librarian: The how and the why—illustrated by case studies from India and Canada. Paper presented at World Library and Information Congress: 75th IFLA General Conference and Council, Milan, Italy.

Davenport, T. H. 1997. *Information ecology: Mastering the information and knowledge environment*. New York: Oxford University Press.

Davenport, T. H., and L. Prusak. 1993. Blow up the corporate library. *International Journal of Information Management* 13: 405–412.

De Rosa, C. 2005. *Perceptions of libraries and information resources: A report to the OCLC membership*. Dublin, OH: OCLC Online Computer Library Center.

Drucker, P. 1999. Knowledge-worker productivity: The biggest challenge. *California Management Review* 41 (2): 79–94.

Drucker, P. F. 1998. The next information revolution. *Forbes ASAP* (Aug. 24).

Drucker, P. F., and J. A. Maciariello. 2004. *The daily Drucker*. New York: HarperCollins.

Friedman, T. L. 2005. *The world is flat: A brief history of the twenty-first century*. New York: Farrar, Straus and Giroux.

Green, S. S. 1876. Personal relations between librarians and readers. *Library Journal* 1 (October): 74–81.

Katzenbach, J. R., and D. K. Smith. 1993. *The wisdom of teams*. New York: HarperCollins.

Page, S. E. 2007. *The difference: How the power of diversity creates better groups, firms, schools, and societies*. Princeton, NJ: Princeton University Press.

Pink, D. H. 2006. *A whole new mind: Why right-brainers will rule the future*. New York: Riverhead Books.

Shumaker, D., and M. Talley. 2009. *Models of embedded librarianship: Final report*. Alexandria, VA: Special Libraries Association.

Taylor, R. S. 1968. Question negotiation and information seeking in libraries. *College & Research Libraries* 29 (3): 178–194.

Tenopir, C., and D. W. King. 2004. *Communication patterns of engineers*. Hoboken, NJ: Wiley.

Chapter 3

Embedded Librarians in Higher Education

Nobue Matsuoka-Motley, Mia Lamm and Nicole Covone, and Gordon Muir and Holly Heller-Ross, profiled in Chapter 1, are just a few of the many academic librarians who have developed embedded roles for themselves. Embedded librarians are working in all sorts of higher learning environments, from 2-year community colleges and technical institutes to professional schools and PhD programs. They are working in traditional classrooms and distance learning environments and in subjects as diverse as culinary arts, performing arts, biology, and engineering, as well as English and history. While no comprehensive census of academic embedded librarians exists, their numbers seem to be significant and growing.

This chapter explores the origins of embedded librarianship in higher education, as well as the different institutional and learning environments in which embedded librarians work, the roles and functions they perform, and some common practices of those who have attained success. It closes with some thoughts on the future and a vision for embedded librarians in academe.

Subject Librarians, Liaison Librarians, and the Origin of Embedded Librarianship

Academic libraries have had positions for *subject librarians* and *liaison librarians* for years. These positions frequently were associated with specialized branch libraries, and the branches were colocated with academic departments to provide convenient access to subject-specific collections. These positions have been common at least since the mid-20th century. In her review of the literature, Margaret Feetham (2006) dated the origins of subject specialist librarians to the University College London during the early 1900s. Within a few decades, these librarians were well-established in Great Britain and the U.S., and their work has been described in a significant body of professional literature.

The primary role of liaison and subject specialist librarians has been collection development. A consensus exists that they must engage in outreach and relationship building, but the main objective has been to obtain faculty input on the specialized library's collections. The American Library Association's *Glossary of Library and Information Science* defined a subject specialist librarian as "a library staff member with superior knowledge of a subject or discipline, with responsibilities for the selection and evaluation of the library's materials in the subject areas and sometimes with the added responsibilities of information service in the subject area and the bibliographic organization of the materials" (Young and Belanger, 1983). Feetham (2006) noted that one subject specialist in 1975 boasted that the quality of the library's collection was his primary achievement, and Stoddart, et al. (2006) pointed out that "traditionally, library outreach and liaison work have focused on collection development" (p. 420).

The emphasis on the collection development role continues to this day. The Reference and User Services Association of the American Library Association published a revision of its *Guidelines for Liaison Work in Managing Collections and Services* in 2010. The title alone conveys the emphasis on collection development, but the text is even more emphatic. Section 3, Definition of Liaison Work, began, "Liaison work is the process by which librarians involve the library's clientele in the assessment of collection needs and services and the measurement of user satisfaction with the collection" (p. 97). The rest of the document continued in that vein, giving no hint that the liaison should have any other goal than collection development.

In practice, there are exceptions to the narrow focus on collection development. Some subject specialist librarians have taken a more holistic approach. Rudasill (2010) noted that reference, instruction, and cataloging were sometimes included in their duties, and they became professionals "who could do it all in a distinct subject area" (p. 83). A study of the duties of subject librarians in the U.K. found that reference work and information literacy instruction were just as common as collection development tasks (Hardy and Corrall, 2007, p. 84). In a study of university library subject specialists, McAbee and Graham found that the subject specialists actually ranked general reference desk service as their most highly valued activity, followed by library instruction, reference provided in office consultations, and then collection development, followed by liai-son to faculty departments (McAbee and Graham, 2005).

Still, whether "do it all" subject specialists or collection development–oriented liaison librarians, the librarians in these roles generally lack the essential characteristics of embedded librarianship. The subject specialist focuses on the subject matter and traditional library roles. If a teaching role exists, it doesn't appear to be well defined. There is no indication that the instruction is embedded into the curriculum, aligned with course assign-ments, or co-taught with subject faculty. The liaison librarian is supposed to form relationships, but only for the purpose of collection develop-ment—there is no sense of reciprocity, no emphasis on the librarian's mak-ing a direct contribution to the teaching, research, or service activities of the faculty. The concept of librarians delivering specific, high-value-added contributions to the work of the subject department, such as co-teaching or performing literature research and analysis, is nonexistent. For the liai-son, traditional roles alone are assumed to be enough, and the primary value is the library—assuming the faculty and students use it—and not in the librarian's professional skills. There's no belief that the subject special-ist or liaison librarian and the subject department share responsibility for outcomes. The orientation is passive and limited. This view fails to exploit the opportunities presented by the librarian's colocation with subject fac-ulty and merely exports traditional library practices to a different location. As Rudasill (2010) concluded, the essence of the difference is that the embedded librarian "is sharing in the life of the department or program," while the subject specialist and liaison roles are not (p. 84).

Despite the weakness of this official and traditional interpretation of the work of subject specialist and liaison librarians, some individuals have extended their role in the direction of embedded librarianship. Stoddart, et al. (2006) recommended taking a role in information literacy instruc-tion and offering in-depth research consultation, although they stopped short of defining a truly embedded approach. Feetham (2006) noted that the term *tutor librarian* was used in the U.K. as early as the 1960s, in recognition of the subject specialist librarian's value as an instructor, not just as a steward of the collection. Some subject specialists have even adopted the term *embedded* to describe their efforts. Proctor, Wartho, and Anderson (2005) described a collaboration between a social science sub-ject specialist librarian and sociology faculty at the University of Otago (New Zealand) to embed information literacy instruction in the curricu-lum for first- and third-year students. Clearly, some innovative subject specialists and liaison librarians have recognized that their positions are leading in the direction of embedded librarianship, even though the official guidelines for the profession fail to recognize the trend.

The Teaching Role of Embedded Librarians

In higher education, embedded librarians teach. The teaching role is so dominant that some authors write about *embedded instruction*, not embedded librarians. Librarians are teaching at all levels (lower undergraduate, upper-level undergraduate, and postgraduate), in all types of institutions, in a wide variety of disciplines, in face-to-face classrooms and in distance education based in virtual learning environments, and with varying levels of collaboration with subject faculty. In this section, we will sample some of this diversity.

Embedded Librarians in 2-Year Institutions

Two-year institutions, such as U.S. community and junior colleges, have been some of the most hospitable to embedded librarianship. The usual focus of these institutions is their instructional mission, and faculty research is not an equal priority. As a result, the contributions of librarians involve information literacy instruction. Some of them have moved quite quickly into embedded instruction.

Information literacy and bibliographic instruction are most effective when they are related to specific courses and assignments. Students are able to apply the concepts and methods from their information literacy instruction immediately to course assignments, and instructors are able to evaluate students' information literacy as a factor in their overall grading of the assignments.

At the Bucks County (PA) Community College, information literacy instruction evolved rapidly in the period from 2007 to 2010. Before 2007, it "consisted mainly of individual 'one-shot' bibliographic instruction sessions with little continuity" and was "not well integrated into the students' course work" (Hemmig and Montet, 2010, p. 658). After attending an institute sponsored by the Association of College and Research Libraries, the community college's information literacy librarian developed a mission statement and set of requirements and implemented a learning-centered program for face-to-face instruction. The program included the following provisions:

- Faculty would provide a course assignment that students would work on at the time they participated in information literacy instruction.
- Faculty would engage their classes in multiple sessions, not just a single "one-shot" instruction program.
- Instruction librarians would customize their presentations for the class level, the subject matter, and the specific assignment.
- There would be targeted courses with standardized formats and assignments, and librarians would collaborate with subject faculty to design assignments and information literacy instruction for these classes. The courses standardized in this manner were required: English Composition and Effective Speaking.
- The instruction librarian and a psychology professor collaborated on a 3-day workshop on information literacy for subject faculty, incorporating principles and processes for developing effective assignments to teach information literacy skills (Hemmig and Montet, 2010).

Building on these steps, the instruction librarian also began to consult more widely with subject faculty and to participate in other in-house professional development forums. Ultimately, the new program of face-to-face embedded instruction became a robust component of the college's curriculum—but this success highlighted the fact that there was no comparable component for its distance learning courses.

To develop its embedded instruction for distance learning courses, the Bucks County library staff followed a model previously developed by the Community College of Vermont. This model relies on asynchronous instruction rather than real-time sessions. Its course management system or virtual learning environment includes a discussion area for research questions, and web-based information literacy tutorials focused on the course level, content, and specific assignment (Matthew and Schroeder, 2006).

Bucks County Community College rolled out its pilot distance education information literacy program with the collaboration of the same psychology professor who had joined in earlier efforts. Ultimately, it was made available to all faculty and courses. Use of new technologies has broadened the scope of the tutorials the librarians can offer, and student use of the resources has expanded. Hemmig and Montet (2010) stressed a key to the program's success:

> Interactivity is the critical element in a successful library presence in online courses. This includes collaboration between librarians and online learning staff, between librarians and online classroom faculty and, most important, direct collaboration between online students and the virtual library. (p. 668)

The experience of Rio Salado College provides an even earlier example of embedded information literacy instruction. Rio Salado is part of the community (2-year) college system of Maricopa County, Arizona. Founded in 1978, it operates without a dedicated campus, primarily as a distance education institution. In 2001, it had only 26 permanent faculty members, along with more than 700 adjunct faculty, to meet the instructional needs of 9,400 full-time students. Most of the 26 permanent faculty, including the library director, operated as academic department heads. Because of the small number of faculty and the close proximity of their offices, the school enjoys a strong collaborative culture. One such collaboration took place when the college gained permission to offer teacher certification programs to individuals who had already obtained their bachelor's degree. Information literacy learning objectives were incorporated into the curriculum, and the library director took responsibility for integrating information literacy modules into the six courses that comprised the program. Course assignments built on the information literacy instruction, and student evaluations included assessment of the information literacy objectives (Davis, 2002).

Embedded Instruction in Bachelor's, Graduate, and Professional Programs

In institutions that grant bachelor's degrees and those that offer graduate and professional education, the faculty teaching mission is balanced by research priorities and other service work. Still, the literature indicates that the primary focus of embedded librarianship at these institutions is the instructional mission. The extent and diversity of embedded information literacy instruction in 4-year, graduate, and professional programs are mind-boggling. Information literacy is embedded in a wide array of disciplines at all academic levels, from first-year undergraduate to PhD. Even setting aside medicine and allied health sciences, covered in Chapter 6, the list of these initiatives is lengthy. Table 3.1 provides an extensive, but by no means exhaustive, inventory of the programs described in the English-language professional literature between 2000 and 2011. (In the table, "Year" refers to the year of publication. Full citations for all publications are given in the Recommended Reading list at www.embedded librarian.com.)

Table 3.1   A Sampling of Embedded Information Literacy Instruction Initiatives, 2000–2011

Authors	Institution	Year	Level	Subject
Black, Crest, Volland	Towson University	2001	Undergraduate	English
Lillard, Wilson, Baird	University of Kentucky	2004	Graduate	Library Science
Hooks, Corbett	Indiana University of Pennsylvania	2005	Graduate	Education
Foutch	Vanderbilt University	2007	First year undergraduate	Human and Organizational Development
Stewart	Pulaski Technical College	2007	Undergraduate	Composition
Bowler, Street	Mount Royal College	2008	Undergraduate	History, Women's Studies
Bozeman, Owens	University of Central Florida, Daytona State College	2008	Undergraduate	Management and other
Deitering, Jameson	Oregon State University	2008	First year undergraduate	Composition
Dugan	Purdue University	2008	Upper level undergraduate	Agricultural Economics
Forrer-Vincent, Carello	University of Colorado	2008	First year undergraduate	Biology
Floyd, Colvin, Bodur	Florida State University	2008	Undergraduate	Education
Hall	Penn State University–Erie	2008	First year undergraduate	Speech
Owens	Daytona Beach College	2008	Undergraduate	Business Writing
Zoellner, Samson, Hines	University of Montana	2008	First year undergraduate	Speech
Beutter Manus	Vanderbilt University	2009	First year undergraduate	Music
Cannon, Jarson	Muhlenberg College	2009	Undergraduate	Writing
Gaspar, Wetzel	George Washington University	2009	Undergraduate	Writing

Authors	Institution	Year	Level	Subject
Herring, Burkhardt, Wolfe	Athens State University	2009	Upper level undergraduate	Multiple
Strahan, Puncochar, Tompkins	Northern Michigan University	2009	Undergraduate and graduate	Multiple
Winterman	Indiana University	2009	Upper level undergraduate	Biology
York	Middle Tennessee State University	2009	Undergraduate and graduate	Multiple
Bennett, Simning	Capella University	2010	Graduate	Psychology
Berdish, Seeman	University of Michigan	2010	Graduate	Business Administration
Betty, Garnar	Regis University	2010	Undergraduate	Multiple
Clark, Chinburg	Rogers State University	2010	Undergraduate	Management Information Systems
Covone, Lamm	Johnson & Wales University	2010	Undergraduate	Culinary Arts
Daly	Duke University	2010	Undergraduate	Multiple
Davis, Smith	University of Central Missouri	2010	Undergraduate	English Composition
Edwards, Kumar, Ochoa	University of Florida	2010	Graduate	Education
Fisher, Heaney	University of Wyoming	2010	First year undergraduate	Interdisciplinary
Garson, McGowan	Harvard University	2010	PhD	Education
Hoffman, Ramin	University of North Texas	2010	Graduate	Library Science
Jacobs	California State University, Stanislaus	2010	Graduate	Education
Kobzina	University of California, Berkeley	2010	Undergraduate	Environmental Studies
Krkoska, Andrews, Morris-Knower	Cornell University	2010	Undergraduate	Biology, Business, Communication
McMillen, Fabbi	University of Nevada, Las Vegas	2010	Upper level undergraduate	Education
Muir, Heller-Ross	State University of New York, Plattsburgh	2010	Upper level undergraduate	Biology
Tumbleson, Burke	Miami University (Ohio)	2010	Undergraduate	Not specified
Weaver, Pier	Wartburg College	2010	First year undergraduate	Oral Communication
Fuselier, Nelson	Minnesota State University	2011	First year undergraduate	Biology
Gronemyer, Dollar	Oregon State University	2011	Upper level undergraduate	Speech Communication
Milne, Thomas	Queensland University of Technology	2011	First year undergraduate	Faculty of Built Environment and Engineering

These examples represent different levels of engagement and different approaches to delivering instruction. In some cases, there is close collaboration between subject faculty and librarians: They create the syllabus together, design assignments that combine subject learning with the application of information literacy skills, share teaching responsibilities, and collaboratively grade papers. In other cases, the librarian is an addition to the course—even if a welcome and valued addition—rather than a full partner in it. In some of these cases, the librarian "attends" classes, in person or virtually, presents one or more lessons, participates in discussions, and serves as a consultant to the students. In still others, instruction is delivered by means of standardized, self-paced modules, which may be accessed from a course management site. The librarian initiates discussion of information literacy topics and responds to student questions.

Shank and Dewald (2003) characterized the different approaches to embedded information literacy instruction as *micro* and *macro*, respectively. With online course management systems as their frame of reference, they defined micro involvement as teamwork between librarians and subject faculty that results in customized instruction and resources for each specific course. Macro involvement means creating a standardized library web presence in the course management system that can be linked to or embedded in any course.

Betty and Garnar (2011) provided an example of both approaches in use at Regis University. Where possible, the Regis librarians initiate collaboration with subject faculty and take an active role in individual courses. They tailor information literacy instruction to course content and individual assignments, and they interact with students individually. This is the *micro* approach. When the micro approach isn't possible, they work with faculty and instructional design staff to create standalone content that instructors can include in their syllabi and course management systems.

At Cornell University, the model for embedded instruction is a five-stage approach. In part, a sequential model for developing the embedded librarianship program, the stages coexist, so that it also serves as a framework for the variety of approaches that can be followed. It starts with Introductory Steps, in which the emphasis is on relationship building, not on collaboration, to achieve specific goals. Then it moves to Awareness, in which resources and services are offered to meet the needs of a broad community. At Cornell, this took the form of a resource for a large group of students in the Applied Economic & Management (AEM) curriculum. From there, it builds to Timely Instructional Services, so-called one-shot information literacy lectures supplemented by virtual reference consultations. At the next level, Partnership, the librarian, faculty, and others work together to obtain, support, and instruct students in the use of important information resources—in the Cornell case, the Bloomberg financial information services. Last, Information Competency involves close collaboration between librarian and faculty to establish appropriate learning goals, integrate multiple learning activities into the subject matter of a course, and evaluate information literacy outcomes (Krkoska, Andrews, and Morris-Knower, 2011).

Embedding in Curriculum Development

The examples and approaches to embedded information literacy instruction described so far are tactical. Whether micro or macro, to use the terminology of Shank and Dewald, they focus on delivering information literacy instruction on a course-by-course basis. These course engagements sometimes come about because of outreach by librarians, and sometimes they result from initiatives by teaching faculty, who recognize the gaps in their students' skills.

There is a level of strategic, embedded information literacy teaching that transcends these course-by-course engagements and can make them more effective. It consists of embedding at the highest level of curriculum development of the institution. When the senior academic officers convene committees and panels to define the overall educational objectives of the institution and the key learning goals of its students, the librarians need to have the relationships and professional credibility to become embedded in them, just as they become embedded in individual courses. By doing so, they can voice the importance of information literacy, a basic tenet of which is learning how to learn, and can lead its informed consideration as one of the main points in the institution's educational strategy. They can also provide leadership in implementing the instructional program. This means collaborating with subject faculty to identify the most appropriate insertion points for embedded information literacy instruction. Following this process transforms embedded instruction from an ad hoc activity that is often under the radar of the institution's leaders—and therefore not highly valued—into a cornerstone of the institution's academic mission.

Some forward-looking institutions, and their librarians, are taking this approach. At a technological university described by Shumaker and Talley (2009), a newly hired librarian volunteered to serve on a universitywide team charged with developing a new course of study for first-year students. The team incorporated information literacy instruction into its recommendation, and the librarian pioneered it. In a follow-up piece, Shumaker (2011) reported that the embedded instruction program expanded from a pilot program that reached only a fraction of the first-year participants into a full-scale program embedded into all sections and reaching all students who enrolled in the special first-year course. In another case, the chief academic officer of a statewide community college system asked the library manager to join the academic council, in large part to give voice to information literacy concerns and to help chart the strategic approach to embedding information literacy instruction most effectively at the right points in the curriculum.

A for-profit U.S. university has taken the systematization of the curriculum development process even further. The library director participates in senior university decision making about curricular objectives, and librarians participate in curriculum development teams that review courses and make changes in course websites and instructional materials. In this way, the librarians are embedded in the full range of curriculum development activities. They have integrated the strategic and tactical elements so that they can influence both high-level direction and tactical implementation, with the goal of delivering the optimal level of information literacy instruction within the curriculum (Shumaker, 2011).

Best Practices for Embedded Instruction

In publications describing their embedded instruction initiatives, authors often include their best practices and recommendations for success. Two approaches of note are those of Chesnut, Wesley, and Zai (2010) and of Hoffman and Ramin (2010). Synthesizing the two yields the following list of recommendations in the areas of technology use, library management and staff involvement, and collaboration with faculty.

Technology

Embedded librarians must ensure that information literacy instruction uses the same technology that the instructor and students are using for other course activities. Unless the librarian's contributions are integrated into the course environment, it's unlikely that either faculty or students will ever visit them. Furthermore, the use of course management systems is becoming increasingly common, not only for distance education, but also as a component of blended and face-to-face instruction. It is becoming increasingly difficult to imagine embedded instruction that lacks a presence in the course's technical infrastructure.

At the same time, if there are multiple embedded librarians in an institution, technology is an important part of their coordination efforts. If the librarians are all using the same infrastructure to develop instructional modules and learning objects, then they can share these objects and reduce the development time and effort required of each librarian.

Library Management and Staff Involvement

Sometimes embedded instruction begins as a relationship between one subject faculty member and one librarian. However, if it is to grow and become a sustained element of the library organization's contribution to the institution's teaching mission, then the engagement of the library management and staff is essential. Without them, the successful go-it-alone librarian quickly runs into the double agony of escalating demands for embedded contributions, on one hand, and conflicts between the embedded role and other duties, on the other. Library management buy-in, and preferably leadership, is essential to the reallocation of duties among staff. Few embedded librarians in higher education report receiving authorization to hire squads of new librarians to pursue embedded engagements. The time spent on embedded instruction has to come from somewhere and often involves a realignment of staff away from the reference desk or other duties. In some cases, lower-skilled staff or even student workers have been substituted for professional reference librarians at the library reference desk. This substitution can make sense from a service point of view, as well as an economic one, provided that part of the embedded librarian's job is to provide research counseling and assistance. Students in classes that engage an embedded librarian contact "their" librarian for help and are, thus, diverted from the reference desk.

Collaboration With Faculty

Embedding information literacy instruction is not something that is done *to* a course, an instructor, or a group of students. If it is to succeed, it must be done *with* them. Hoffman and Ramin (2010) in particular recognized this and highlighted the importance of collaboration with faculty. They advocated active marketing of the embedded role to instructors and negotiation to establish clear expectations for the librarian's participation. When agreement is achieved, the librarian must prepare by becoming familiar with the course material, instructional objectives, and specific assignments. Following along with the emphasis on technology integration already discussed, Hoffman and Ramin advocated that the librarian obtain read and write permissions for the course management system. Once the course begins, the librarian may be introduced by the subject instructor and should immediately take an active role, initiating discussions and posting recommendations, as well as being a contributor and responding reliably and promptly to student questions.

Beyond the Teaching Role

Some embedded librarians in higher education do more than teach. There are fewer reports in the literature from academic librarians embedded in nonteaching activities, but in some ways, their experiences are even more diverse than those who are involved in information literacy instruction.

At Arizona State University, Christopher Miller (2011) became an embedded librarian in the School of Dance when the school received a gift of an important special collection, along with an endowment to support a dedicated (embedded) curator–librarian. Miller summarized his experience as being "completely integrated into the department and its processes"—being viewed and treated as a departmental colleague. He has input into the curriculum and is able to advocate successfully for the inclusion of information literacy, and he influences other information management issues and participates in fundraising and grant writing.

Miller offers two examples of his engagement. One is his collaboration with the school administration to document the residency of a visiting choreographer. The second, even more far-reaching, is the "e-kiNETx" project. In this project, he is working with faculty and the school's administration to develop a retrieval system based on movement: By performing a motion, the information seeker will be able to retrieve related information objects.

At the same time, Miller provides a range of instructional and research services. For example, he opened his essay with a classic experience of embedded librarians. Overhearing the frustration of a dance student having little success with her research, he came to the rescue unbidden, helping her with her project while communicating in a language consisting of a mix of words and movement.

Continuing with a performing arts focus, Matsuoka-Motley (Matos, Matsuoka-Motley, and Mayer, 2010) described the multiple dimensions of her role as embedded librarian in the Department of Performing Arts of the American University in Washington, D.C. Her role, like Miller's, began with a broader initiative: in this case, a new building, the Katzen Center for the Performing Arts. The university librarian was able to obtain office space in the department's section of the building, and Matsuoka-Motley took up full-time residence there. Her activities include information literacy instruction, collaboration on other teaching and scholarship initiatives, coaching performing arts students, and serving as a panel judge for jury exams. She notes that circulation of the performing arts library's resources has jumped during the period that she has been embedded and developing relationships in the department.

Some embedded librarians focus specifically on collaboration in research projects. Carlson and Kneale (2011) described this approach at Purdue University. In this model, librarians did not engage with a single department or academic discipline but sought to become embedded in projects based on their affinity with the project (and perhaps past relationships with the researchers). This approach has the advantage of aligning well with the increasingly interdisciplinary nature of academic research, because the librarians are not limited to work with a single unit. Carlson and Kneale offered a variety of roles that the embedded librarian can play in these engagements, such as preparing data for dissemination beyond the project team, preparing the data for preservation, and "designing workflows and systems to organize, manage, and deliver project documentation or other needed materials" (p. 168). In other words, the librarian has the potential to contribute in a variety of ways, not simply through reference, research, document delivery, or news alerting.

Carlson and Kneale (2011) contrasted the Purdue project-oriented model with what they termed a *programmatic* approach, exemplified by a university-affiliated specialized research institute, the National Solar Observatory. In this model, the research organization hires the embedded librarian, who reports not to a parent centralized library facility but to the research organization. A similar approach was described by Tara Murray (2010) in the DIY Librarian blog. Robinson-Garcia and Torres-Salinas (2011) also argued for greater emphasis on the opportunities for embedded librarians in academic research projects. They recommended five distinct roles for these librarians:

- Managing the publication of papers from the team's research
- Serving as the team's publicity agent: disseminating publications, results, and news of activities; managing the team's website
- Organizing and preserving the team's data and other research artifacts
- Managing resources used by the team, whether information resources, curriculum management systems, grant and project application forms, or others
- Monitoring and publicizing the results of the team's publications and activities; generating bibliometric reports, and advising team members regarding research and publication policies

The roles of embedded librarians are often tailored, not just to circumstances at a particular institution, but to a variety of needs within different units of an institution. Jezmynne Dene (2011) and Linda Bartnik, et al. (2010) described two such multiphase, multidimensional initiatives.

At the Claremont Colleges (Dene, 2011), embedded engagements include partnering with the coordinator of the Writing Center to ensure that information literacy coaching is part of the guidance given to students seeking writing help. In addition, a librarian embedded with the team responsible for the Colleges' course management system made a variety of information resources and instructional modules available as an integrated capability of the system. The success of this system-level initiative led to requests by faculty for information literacy instruction and for librarians to be embedded in specific courses. Finally, in a third phase of the embedded librarianship initiative, embedded librarians were assigned a broad range of tasks, including the following:

- Integrating into the community; spending time away from the library
- Teaching classes
- Establishing relationships, sharing resources with the community, and reporting community news back to the library organization
- Participating in campus committees and groups

- Providing reference assistance
- Maintaining a virtual presence to serve the community

In an article by Bartnik, et al. (2010), Bartnik describes her experiences and the development of multiple roles as an embedded librarian. She was welcomed by and strongly embedded into the College of Business. During a 3-year period, her roles grew to include the following:

- Serving as a committee member and presenter for the college's professional development seminars
- Participating in tours for faculty position candidates
- Acting as a unit "director" for an accreditation team's visit
- Making classroom presentations
- Accessing and using the college's email list and shared server
- Being added to course pages in the course management system
- Serving as an ad hoc committee member for several college committees

Unfortunately, Bartnik became a victim of her own success. Promoted to head of the library's reference department, she found it impossible to maintain the time and attention needed to continue her embedded activities and experienced a dramatic slippage of her involvement in the college.

How to Succeed—And What to Watch Out For

Given the range and development of embedded librarianship in the teaching and research missions of higher education, it's not surprising that librarians encounter resistance, obstacles, and pitfalls. For those contemplating an initiative, it can be helpful to understand what works—that is, the common practices of those who have succeeded. Several authors have shared some of the problems and pitfalls, while others have recommended best practices.

Problems and Pitfalls

In higher education, librarians who develop closer relationships with faculty groups or research groups dilute their relationships with central

library staff and operations. Embedded librarians have experienced problems and pitfalls with both sets of relationships. Here is a brief survey of
these concerns, followed by a summary of some corresponding best practices; Chapter 9 provides a fuller treatment of problems and best practices.

The most common complaint is that subject faculty members resist the
idea of partnerships with librarians. Most important, some instructors
don't wish to cede class time or content to information literacy topics,
because they are preoccupied with their course subject material and don't
see the value of embedded information literacy instruction. Other forms
of resistance have to do with allocating space for the embedded librarian
or making other commitments, such as funding and inclusion in meetings, activities, and initiatives.

At the other end of the spectrum, embedded librarians—especially
those who move out of a centralized library full-time—mourn the loss of
communication and collaboration with their librarian friends and colleagues. Miller (2011) noted that "all significant challenges that I have
encountered personally in my embedded experience filter down into variations of isolation from other library and information professionals" (p.
103). This isolation can have repercussions beyond social contact and
emotional support. It can inhibit knowledge sharing and affect the librarian's performance evaluation. Several writers have noted that central
library managers and colleagues don't gain firsthand knowledge of the
embedded librarian's accomplishments, while the faculty with which the
librarian is embedded lack the background to make an independent evaluation of the librarian's work.

The experiences of Bartnik, et al. (2010) illustrate the range of challenges that embedded librarians encounter. Although Bartnik herself
enjoyed great success, as described earlier, another librarian's work with
the College of Education was slowed by the faculty's aversion to change
and continued reliance on a prior arrangement in which suboptimal
information services were provided by a member of the Education faculty,
not integrated with library operations. In this case, office politics and simple resistance to change were overcome through persistence and
patience.

In a third example (Bartnik, et al., 2010), a librarian assigned to build
relationships with the College of Science, Engineering, and Technology
had to overcome decades of poor communication between the College
and the library. A history of bad feeling can mean that the fresh librarian

who arrives on the scene and announces a new dawn is greeted with skepticism, if not outright hostility.

A fourth colleague pursued a strategy of physical colocation to develop visibility and relationships. To maximize visibility, she would position herself in different department lobbies, post a sign that "The Librarian Is IN!," and invite questions and conversation. The lack of privacy in lobby situations and the inconvenient layout and position of some of them inhibited her success. Although she developed excellent social relationships and engaged in important conversation, she was less successful in expanding her direct contributions to the work of the college. She concluded, "Even though the amount of questions was never very high, the close proximity and physical presence of the librarian … served as a weekly reminder that friendly help was always available" (Bartnik, et al., 2010, p. 161) In this case, it seems that a real partnership was never formed and that college faculty members were never truly engaged or committed to working with the librarian. As a result, visibility and social relationships, while important, did not lead to deeper collaboration, at least during the time frame covered by the report. Her experience suggests that establishing shared goals and collaborating to achieve them must accompany the development of communication and social relationships. The latter alone are not enough.

Best Practices

Common threads among the "best practices" recommendations of successful embedded academic librarians are listed here.

From Heider (2010):

- Obtain stakeholder buy-in.
- Include faculty in hiring the embedded librarian.
- Look for the following qualities in hiring: leadership skills, ability to advocate for both library and information user group, collaboration and outreach skills, a relevant subject graduate degree, and prior subject work experience.
- Once hired, the librarian should:
  - Maintain a physical presence with information user group.
  - Attend user-group meetings.
  - Serve as subject bibliographer.

- Offer instruction and guest lectures.
- Develop collaborative programs that use library's resources.
- Offer to teach credit courses.
- Publish and present with subject faculty.

From Cooper (2010):

- Eavesdrop (on email lists, etc.).
- Go where the action is, whether office, labs, studios, or elsewhere.
- Create appropriate spaces (which will vary by discipline).
- Use existing events to promote library.
- Respond to the need for current information (provide news alerting).

From Dene (2011):

- Study the information user community.
- Start small and work up from small successes.
- Outline assessment strategies.
- Regularly spend time in a highly visible location.
- Present library resources and services at orientation sessions.
- Collaborate with others, such as the computing department.
- Join faculty or student interest groups.
- Have, and use, an "elevator speech."

From Miller (2011):

- Establish a strong presence in the academic department.
- Seek out conversations.
- Participate in department events.
- Attend professional or scholarly meetings in the discipline, forgoing library conferences if necessary.

All these authors address the importance of active communication and collaboration, as well as the value of physical presence. They present a range of recommendations for learning about the subject matter of the group and understanding the group's operations, contributing to its conversations, and initiating specific projects and services. Notably, none of the recommendations involve waiting to be asked.

Heider (2010) emphasized mutuality and reciprocity and took stakeholder buy-in and participation to the level of including subject faculty in the process of hiring a new embedded librarian. Miller took commitment of the information user group for granted, since his position in the School of Dance was established by a directed endowment. Dene expanded the concept of stakeholder buy-in to include the library administration, which is clearly an important stakeholder. Dene was alone in also including a plan for systematic evaluation of the embedded initiative. In all cases, colocation may be an enabler, but the real key is proactive, substantive engagement. As Cooper (2010) succinctly phrased it, "Every example of embedded librarianship relies on two key elements: relationships and relevance" (p. 323). Neither one is sufficient by itself. The best practices are designed to develop both in tandem.

Opportunities for Embedded Librarians in Higher Education: A Vision

In 1994, the Virginia Polytechnic Institute and State University, more familiarly known as Virginia Tech, began a "College Librarian" program. The new program constituted a major departure from Tech's former, highly centralized library operational structure. Describing the program in a 2002 article, Seamans and Metz set out its revolutionary characteristics:

- It was to be "user- and college-centric by taking the services out of the library and placing them into the colleges" (p. 325).
- A key goal was to be the building of interpersonal relationships between librarians and subject faculty.
- The primary responsibility of the College Librarians would be to the college they served, and not to the library organization.

In pursuing these goals, the College Librarians became more than librarians providing a service—they became colleagues of the academic administrators and subject faculty. Seamans and Metz (2002) wrote as follows:

The role of faculty colleague—of a junior variety in most, but not all, contexts—has come as a largely unanticipated by-product of the college librarians' presence as collabora- tors and neighbors with the teaching faculty. It is not uncommon now for college librarians to attend the regular meetings of department heads with their academic deans, to travel with other faculty to workshops or national meet- ings, or to serve on faculty search committees. A few have participated as coinvestigators on grants. (p. 328)

A decade later, Barbara Dewey (2004), then dean of libraries at the University of Tennessee, issued a far-reaching manifesto in which she asserted the centrality of librarians to the academic enterprise. She noted that librarians, as methodological experts who work across all disciplines and nearly every sector of the university, are uniquely situated to contribute to core and strategic activities. To realize their potential, however, Dewey advocated that librarians embed themselves in all phases of the academic world—research, teaching and learning, and service—and that they step up to volunteer for leadership roles. Embedding can take place not only within academic departments or information literacy instruction initiatives. While those areas are important and valuable, embedding can also take place in strategic planning and other universitywide initiatives, with fundraising and development, and with information technology initiatives.

Dewey (2004) concluded:

The embedded librarian, who is truly integrated into the aca- demic, administrative, athletic, cultural, research, teaching, and learning arenas of the university, provides quality and depth to the total campus experience. ... Recognition of the power of embedding, integrating, and collaborating leads to amazing innovations in the academy that would not exist without the influence and leadership of librarians. (p. 16)

The vision of embedded librarianship has since been picked up by some authors. For instance, in his 2007 article, "A Strategy for Academic Libraries in the First Quarter of the 21st Century," David Lewis included this imperative in his five-point strategy: "Reposition library and informa- tion tools, resources, and expertise so that they are embedded into the teaching, learning, and research enterprises" (p. 420). In elaborating on this point, however, Lewis revealed a degree of uncertainty and ambiguity in his vision. He advocated strengthening personal interactions and relationships between librarians and information users and recognized that neither the traditional reference desk model nor the augmented virtual reference model will be sufficient to achieve this end. However, he confessed, "it is unclear to me what alternatives will work best" (p. 425) and gives no hint of the path to an embedded librarianship model. Other authoritative authors have given even less attention to the embedded model. In their 2006 and 2009 reports (published in 2008 and 2010, respectively) on faculty information behavior for the ITHAKA organization, Housewright and Schonfeld (2008; Schonfeld and Housewright, 2010) never mentioned embedded librarians, although they did allow the word *informationists* to creep into their 2009 report. They conceived of librarians only as "gatekeepers" and never asked questions about librarians as collaborators or partners in any aspect of the teaching or research missions. Most fundamentally, they were preoccupied with libraries as institutions and did not admit into their worldview the idea of librarians as professionals distinct from the library's institutional identity. In short, they did not take into account the viewpoints and lessons of Seamans and Metz (2002), Dewey (2004), and the many others who have described successes.

It has been more than half a century since the subject liaison librarian became established in the profession, and nearly 20 years since the first truly embedded librarians in higher education began to revolutionize their relationship to the rest of the academic enterprise. In the past decade, interest in embedded librarianship has exploded, and the number of initiatives has proliferated. Some are bold; some are mild. Many have been successful; others have not. They offer important opportunities for academic librarians in the coming years but continue to face obstacles. The skepticism and resistance of faculty and academic administrators will continue to be obstacles that innovative librarians will have to overcome. But the greater obstacle will be the ingrained limitations of the vision and ambitions of many in the academic library establishment.

Summary

Embedded librarianship in higher education proceeds from a longer tradition of subject liaison librarians, but transcends that tradition in important ways. It focuses on collaboration to achieve shared institutional goals in teaching and research, not on traditional reference service and collection development consultation.

At every level, and in every type of higher education institution, embedded librarians are focusing overwhelmingly on information literacy instruction. They are working with subject faculty in a wide variety of disciplines: in the humanities, social sciences, natural sciences, and professional schools. They are embedding information literacy into classroom instruction and virtual or distance education. They are involved in introductory courses for first-year students, advanced seminars for upper-division undergraduates, and at all levels of graduate education up to and including PhD programs. They are shaping research assignments, presenting lectures and conducting class exercises, creating self-paced tutorials embedded in courseware, and even participating in the grading of student work.

Some embedded librarians have moved from tactical engagement with specific courses and individual academic units to strategic engagement with the institutional curriculum development process. They collaborate with the academic leadership to embed information literacy instruction at key points in the curriculum, where it will reach the maximum number of students and have the greatest effect.

Other librarians have begun to move beyond the instructional role. They are beginning to find needs for collaboration on research, information gathering and analysis, and data management to advance the academic research goal.

Still, not all embedded librarianship initiatives are successful. Many librarians confront stereotypes, indifference, and the legacy of past institutional conflicts. The available accounts of these difficulties suggest that relationship building is necessary, but not sufficient, to overcome these obstacles. The ability to define clear, mutual goals that are aligned with the institutional mission, and then deliver successfully on the promise of improved performance, is also of the essence.

At this juncture, the future of embedded librarianship in higher education is promising. As we learn from the successful pioneers, more academic librarians can establish collaborative relationships in the teaching mission, and explore other opportunities to contribute to research and service as well.

References

Bartnik, L., K. Farmer, A. Ireland, L. Murray, and J. Robinson. 2010. We will be assimilated: Five experiences in embedded librarianship. *Public Services Quarterly* 6: 150–164.

Betty, P., and M. Garnar. 2011. One university, two approaches: The Regis experience with embedded librarianship. In *Embedded librarians: Moving beyond one-shot instruction.*, eds. C. Kvenild and K. Calkins, 139–153. Chicago: Association of College and Research Libraries.

Carlson, J., and R. Kneale. 2011. Embedded librarianship in the research context: Navigating new waters. *College & Research Libraries News* 72 (3): 167–170.

Chesnut, M. T., T. L. Wesley, and R. Zai. 2010. Adding an extra helping of service when you already have a full plate: Building an embedded librarian program. *Public Services Quarterly* 6: 122–129.

Cooper, R. A. 2010. Architects in the mist: Embedding the librarian in a culture of design. *Public Services Quarterly* 6 (August): 323–329.

Davis, H. 2002. Information literacy modules as an integral component of a K–12 teacher preparation program: A librarian/faculty partnership. *Journal of Library Administration* 37 (1/2): 207–216.

Dene, J. 2011. Embedded librarianship at the Claremont colleges. In *Embedded librarians: Moving beyond one-shot instruction*, eds. C. Kvenild and K. Calkins, 219–228. Chicago: Association of College and Research Libraries.

Dewey, B. 2004. The embedded librarian: Strategic campus collaborations. *Resource Sharing & Information Networks* 17 (1/2): 5–17.

Feetham, M. 2006. The subject specialist in higher education—A review of the literature. In *Subject librarians: Engaging with the learning and teaching environment*, eds. P. Dale, M. Holland, and M. Matthews, 3–17. Burlington, VT: Ashgate.

Guidelines for liaison work in managing collections and services. 2010. *Reference & User Services Quarterly* 50 (1): 97–98.

Hardy, G., and S. Corrall. 2007. Revisiting the subject librarian: A study of English law and chemistry. *Journal of Libraries & Information Science* 39 (2): 79–91.

Heider, K. L. 2010. Ten tips for implementing a successful embedded librarian program. *Public Services Quarterly* 6: 110–121.

Hemmig, W., and M. Montet. 2010. The "just for me" virtual library: Enhancing an embedded eBrarian program. *Journal of Library Administration* 50: 657–669.

Hoffman, S., and L. Ramin. 2010. Best practices for librarians embedded in online courses. *Public Services Quarterly* 6: 292–305.

Housewright, R., and R. Schonfeld. 2008. *Ithaka's 2006 studies of key stakeholders in the digital transformation in higher education*. New York: Ithaka.

Krkoska, B. B., C. Andrews, and J. Morris-Knower. 2011. A tale of three disciplines: Embedding librarians and outcomes-based information literacy competency in business, biology, and communication. In *Embedded librarians: Moving beyond one-shot instruction*, eds. C. Kvenild and K. Calkins, 121–130. Chicago: Association of College and Research Libraries.

Lewis, D. W. 2007. A strategy for academic libraries in the first quarter of the 21st century. *College & Research Libraries News* (September): 418–434.

Matos, M. A., N. Matsuoka-Motley, and W. Mayer. 2010. The embedded librarian online or face-to-face: American University's experiences. *Public Services Quarterly* 6: 130–130.

Matthew, V., and A. Schroeder. 2006. The embedded librarian program: Faculty and librarians partner to embed personalized library assistance into online courses. *Educause Quarterly* 4: 61–65.

McAbee, S. L., and J. Graham. 2005. Expectations, realities and perceptions of subject librarians' duties in medium-sized academic libraries. *Journal of Academic Librarianship* 31 (1): 19–28.

Miller, C. 2011. Embedded and embodied: Dance librarianship within the academic department. In *Embedded librarianship: Moving beyond one-shot instruction*, eds. C. Kvenild and K. Calkins, 95–107. Chicago, IL: Association of College and Research Libraries.

Murray, T. 2010. *Embedded library*. Message posted to www.diylibrarian.org/archive/2010/06/30/embedded-library. (Accessed April 20, 2012.)

Proctor, L., R. Wartho, and M. Anderson. 2005. Embedding information literacy in the sociology program at the University of Otago. *Australian Academic & Research Libraries*: 153–168.

Robinson-Garcia, N., and D. Torres-Salinas. 2011. Librarians 'embedded' in research. CILIP Update Gazette, 10 (6): 44–46.

Rudasill, L. M. 2010. Beyond subject specialization: The creation of embedded librarians. *Public Services Quarterly* 6: 83–91.

Schonfeld, R., and R. Housewright. 2010. *Faculty survey 2009: Key strategic insights for libraries, publishers, and societies.* New York: Ithaka.

Seamans, N. H., and P. Metz. 2002. Virginia Tech's innovative college librarian program. *College & Research Libraries* 63 (4): 324–332.

Shank, J. D., and N. H. Dewald. 2003. Establishing our presence in courseware: Adding library services to the virtual classroom. *ITAL: Information Technology and Libraries* 22 (1): 38–43.

Shumaker, D. 2011. *Models of embedded librarianship: Addendum 2011.* Alexandria, VA: Special Libraries Association.

Shumaker, D., and M. Talley. 2009. *Models of embedded librarianship: Final report.* Alexandria, VA: Special Libraries Association.

Stoddart, R. A., T. W. Bryant, A. L. Baker, A. Lee, and B. Spencer. 2006. Going boldly beyond the reference desk: Practical advice and learning plans for new reference libraries performing liaison work. *The Journal of Academic Librarianship* 32 (4): 419–427.

Young, H., and T. Belanger. 1983. *Glossary of library and information science.* Chicago: American Library Association.

Chapter 4

Embedded Librarians
in the Health Sciences

Medical librarians adopted embedded librarianship decades ago, but until recently, they haven't used the term *embedded*. The rich literature that documents their efforts uses terms such as *clinical librarian, informationist, information specialist in context,* and, perhaps borrowed from the higher education sector, *liaison.* But, until recently, hardly ever *embedded.* Still, based on the working definition of the embedded librarian as an "integral part to the whole," a librarian who works closely with a group of information users, develops close working relationships, and delivers high-value, customized information to meet their needs—these medical librarians are indeed embedded. This chapter traces the development of embedded librarianship in the fields of healthcare education and delivery and explores the diversity of contexts and roles in which medical embedded librarians have been engaged. It reviews the lists of best practices that medical librarians have recommended to their colleagues and surveys the work done over decades to evaluate the contributions of embedded librarians in medical education and practice. The chapter closes with some thoughts on the future of embedded librarianship in the health sciences.

Origins

The germ of the idea for embedded librarianship in medicine can be traced back to the 1960s, when the practice of medicine began to be seen as a team activity, not the domain of a solo physician acting alone. Early in the decade, the report "Lifetime Learning for Physicians" (Dryer, 1962), also known as the Dryer Report, documented the gulf between what was known in the literature and what was being applied in medical practice. Also during this decade, the roles of pharmacists, social workers, nurses, nutritionists, and psychologists in clinical care began to receive recognition. In particular, there arose the idea of the clinical pharmacist, who accompanied the medical doctor in visiting patients and contributed specialized knowledge to treatment decisions.

Taking her cue from this trend, Dr. Gertrude Lamb, director of the library at the School of Medicine, University of Missouri–Kansas City, applied for and received a grant to initiate a "clinical medical librarian" program, which ran from 1972 to 1975. Dr. Lamb spoke about her initiative at the Medical Library Association conference in 1972. In the succeeding years, she and others replicated the model of clinical medical librarianship in other medical schools and hospitals (Cimpl, 1985).

The primary goals of these programs were to provide information to the healthcare teams quickly and to influence the healthcare professionals to make more and better use of the literature to inform their decision making and actions. The programs generally involved the librarian in *rounding*, or the process of doctors and other health professionals visiting patients, reviewing their statuses, and discussing diagnostic, treatment, and care questions. Given the technology of the time, the librarian harvested questions from these discussions and then returned to the library to conduct research and to identify and obtain relevant literature. The librarian then provided copies of key documents or summaries of findings to the appropriate members of the healthcare team. In addition, the clinical medical librarians sometimes provided information directly to patients. The program at McMaster University was one in which the clinical medical librarian devoted a significant proportion of time to supplying patient information (Marshall and Neufeld, 1981).

Clinical medical librarianship continued to develop into the 1990s, albeit somewhat slowly, and studies documented its beneficial effects. Still, the problem of applying scientific knowledge in the teaching of health sciences and in medical practice continued to grow. The term *evidence-based medicine* came into use to express the importance of applying evidence from the literature and was expanded into *evidence-based healthcare* to incorporate the recognition that nurses, pharmacists, and all healthcare professionals shared the need to use the literature effectively in their work. Ultimately, the term *evidence-based practice* emerged. Perry and Kronenfeld (2005) have identified these essential steps of the evidence-based model:

- Recognizing and formulating an answerable question
- Locating relevant "knowledge artifacts"
- Critically evaluating them
- Synthesizing an appropriate evidence-based answer from them
- Applying the answer in a collaborative way with the patient

The idea of evidence-based practice according to these steps was attractive, but it wasn't so easy to follow in real life. Critical obstacles included the never-ending time pressures on medical professionals, the tendency of doctors (like most of us) to seek information from other people rather than from documents and databases, and lack of skill in using databases of medical literature (Coumou and Meijman, 2006). By the late 1990s, clinical librarianship had gained recognition at some institutions but was not in wide use. Librarians at institutions such as Vanderbilt University had gained considerable experience. They participated in rounds, capturing explicit questions and also listening for the implied questions that came up as the clinical team discussed the patients. The librarians recognized the importance of expertise and ongoing education in both the specialized subject matter of the clinicians and the use of information retrieval systems. They had conducted some evaluations that provided some validation of the worth of their efforts (Giuse, et al., 1998).

Meanwhile, the need to broaden and systemize the response to the knowledge gap in healthcare remained, and visionaries in the medical library community recognized that more needed to be done. Writing in 1997, Giuse articulated a vision of the clinical librarian as an "equal voice with other specialists who support clinical decision-making," who "project themselves not as information 'servers' who trail the team in an auxiliary capacity, but as an integral part of the group with a specialized expertise that can contribute vitally to clinical situations" (p. 437). The key to achieving this status, she wrote, was to establish a trusted relationship with other members of the team, and the key to establishing trust was to be competent and well-prepared. Giuse advocated that the clinical librarian have a strong "medical knowledge base" in addition to mentored practice in "searching, retrieving, filtering, and summarizing information." Soon, a new proposal would crystallize her recommendations.

Transition: From Clinical Librarian to Informationist

The new proposal came in the form of an *Annals of Internal Medicine* editorial by Frank Davidoff and Valerie Florance (2000). They proposed a new kind of healthcare professional, with a new title: *informationist.*

Davidoff and Florance (2000) took as their starting point the ongoing gap between research and the practice of medicine. "The disappointing reality," they said, "is that physicians still don't regularly search the medical literature themselves, nor do they ask for professional help in searching nearly as often as they need to" (p. 996). Reviewing the 30-year history of clinical medical librarianship, they found that such programs are both efficient and effective, and they advocated that informationists become as widespread in medical care as "head nurses or office managers" (p. 997). The informationist would meet the information needs of every member of the clinical care team, and of patients as well.

Informationists would combine a knowledge of both information science and clinical work, and would be the product of an accredited education and professional certification. They would report to clinical management, and their services would be paid for directly, just as other specialists on the clinical team. Just as attending physicians rely on a range of technical specialists for chemical lab tests, computed tomography scans, and the like, they—and the rest of the clinical team—would rely on informationists to ensure that the best available findings from the literature were informing all aspects of care.

The informationist proposal has fundamentally influenced the field ever since its publication. In an early reaction, Plutchak (2000) recognized its radical nature: "This informationist is a true hybrid—still a librarian, but one steeped in the clinic in a substantially new way" (p. 392). In 2002, the Medical Library Association and the National Library of Medicine held a conference with the aim of developing a consensus definition and an action program to spread the implementation of the informationist concept (Shipman, et al., 2002). Participants wrestled with the issues of finding appropriate recruits; developing the necessary educational and training programs; funding informationist services; marketing the concept to medical administrators; finding opportunities to test and implement it; and assessing its value.

In the ensuing years, the concepts of *clinical medical librarian* and informationist continued to evolve, even as they spread. The Medical Library Association began to use the formulation *information specialist in context* for the new embedded-librarian role. Writing in 2005, Perry and

Kronenfeld proposed a set of expanded roles for librarians in the areas of "engagement at the institutional level in setting the knowledge-based resource use agenda" (p. 14), and specifically the following:

- Building knowledge systems
- Training staff in evidence-based practice
- Building client-centric library services
- Delivering "highly customized, answer-focused mediated knowledge-based search services" (p. 14)
- Collaborating with information technology staff to integrate knowledge and institutional information systems

In a review of the literature, Rankin, Grefsheim, and Canto (2008) found reports from informationists at 15 different institutions, some represented by more than one article, and suggested that two distinct variations of the concept had emerged— the clinical informationist and the bioinformatics informationist. Significant differences between the two stem from their evolution. The clinical informationist began with an emphasis on customized service and the development of a team relationship, found opportunities to deliver credible information, and expanded the depth and sophistication of contributions to the team's work. The bioinformatics informationist, on the other hand, emphasized strong technical skills at the outset and developed customized contributions and strong working relationships over time.

The Medical Library Association has continued to explore and develop the concept ever since, with a special program at its 2010 annual conference (the tenth anniversary of Davidoff and Florance's editorial), the establishment of an interest group, and many other programs.

Contemporary Roles of Embedded Librarians in Healthcare and Health Sciences

Throughout the history of embedded librarianship in healthcare and health sciences—from clinical medical librarian to informationist to information specialist in context—medical librarians take responsibility for providing information to patients, to clinical care teams, and to researchers. They also lead in information literacy instruction at all levels of education, from undergraduate programs in allied healthcare professions, to graduate and doctoral programs, to continuing education for medical professionals. While a few accounts focus exclusively on one of these roles, embedded librarians at most institutions wear a variety of hats.

Information for Patients

Some of the earliest accounts of embedded medical librarians emphasize information delivery to patients. McMaster University in Toronto was a leader in this area. By 1975, Joanne Marshall and others were participating in hospital rounds—as prescribed in Lamb's pioneering work—and preparing information packets to help patients understand the nature of their illness and the treatment they were receiving (Cimpl, 1985; Kates, 1978; Roseman, 1978). The clinical librarian served all members of the healthcare community; patient requests accounted for about a quarter (24 percent) of all requests fielded (Marshall and Neufeld, 1981).

Information for Clinical and Research Teams

Other accounts have focused on research and information analysis for the different professional specialists that make up clinical teams.

At a nonteaching hospital in Harrisburg, Pennsylvania, librarians established a role in the program for medical residents. They provided real-time research and answers to clinical questions during one "morning report" session per week. They found that the program improved the residents' own use of the literature, increased demands for librarians to collaborate, and led to better, more-collegial relationships between residents and the clinical librarians (Coldsmith and Schwing, 2005). Studies of research services provided by clinical librarians and informationists to all medical staff in Brighton, England, and Dublin, Ireland, found good support for the value of the research and its impact on care, as well as a demand for closer collaboration of informationists with the clinical teams (Brookman, et al., 2006; Flynn and McGuinness, 2011).

Taking a different approach, librarians at the University of Sheffield, England, initiated a clinical research service aimed specifically at meeting the needs of the nursing staff. The service was intended to enable the nurses to make better use of evidence from the literature in their patient care. It was the practice for nurses to hold "handover meetings" every afternoon. At these meetings, nurses departing from the day shift would discuss issues with nurses coming in for the evening shift. The librarian arranged to attend these meetings once a week. By participating in these conversations, the librarian would be able to identify information needs and either provide relevant evidence from the literature immediately or follow up later (Tod, et al., 2007).

Information Literacy Instruction

Institutions such as teaching hospitals, as well as undergraduate and graduate programs in health sciences, have teaching missions. In these institutions, clinical librarianship initiatives have emphasized the development of embedded information literacy instruction. At Virginia Commonwealth University in Richmond, Virginia, a professional health sciences librarian was embedded in the School of Medicine, given associate professor rank, and assigned as director of the school's computer-based instruction lab, reporting to the dean, not the library director. The position included responsibility for embedded medical informatics instruction, which was carried out through collaboration with both subject faculty and library staff (Seago, 2004). Similarly, the Faculty of Medicine at Imperial College London established a Medicine Information Literacy Group, which embedded information literacy instruction in the college's curriculum. Information literacy instruction was coordinated with the college's Problem Based Learning curriculum and included such topics as plagiarism and critical appraisal of evidence, in addition to search and retrieval skills (Cousins and Perris, 2009).

In some cases, embedded information literacy instruction in the health sciences is similar to its counterpart in other subjects in higher education, as described in Chapter 3. Ferris State University, in Big Rapids, Michigan, offers online courses in its master's of nursing and healthcare systems administration degrees, and the health sciences librarian is embedded in certain courses in these programs, participating in the courses through the course management system (Konieczny, 2010). At Southeastern Louisiana University, a pilot project in the Foundations of Advanced Nursing course expanded into embedded instruction for a master's of science in nursing program offered by a consortium of three universities (Guillot, Stahr, and Meeker, 2010).

Examples of Sustained Success

Published accounts of their work by several programs of clinical medical librarianship over a number of years provide some insights into the programs' success and progress. The programs include those at the University of Florida Health Science Center, the U.S. National Institutes of Health (NIH), and the Vanderbilt University Eskind Biomedical Library.

The University of Florida Health Science Center refers to its program as a *liaison librarian* program. Begun in 1998, the program sought to establish closer communications and better services with six different colleges that made up the Health Science Center (Tennant, et al., 2001). The liaison plan identified seven areas of focus:

- Communication
- Collection development
- Education
- User services
- Information access
- Liaison development
- Program evaluation

These areas bear a strong resemblance to the more-innovative roles of liaison librarians articulated by academic librarians during this time, as discussed in Chapter 3.

By 2006, some, if not all, of the liaison librarians had significantly outperformed expectations. Two positions, one in nursing and one in a new Genetics Institute, had been cofunded by the respective information user groups, and the librarians were given office space colocated with the staff of these units, away from the library. By the time of an evaluation conducted in 2006, there were nine liaison librarians to the various colleges. The evaluation showed a wide variation in the levels of collaboration achieved by the liaisons: Three had published with subject faculty, two had given presentations at scholarly or professional meetings with subject faculty, one had been given a joint appointment in an academic department, and one had been asked to co-teach a course (Tennant, Cataldo, and Jesano, 2006). The article didn't make clear whether it was the same liaison who was asked to co-teach, received a joint appointment, and was one of those who had co-presented and co-authored. The possibility exists that one or two of the liaisons were very successful and became strongly embedded or whether the successes reported were spread out among the liaison librarians.

In 2008, Tennant, the bioinformatics librarian, and Miyamoto, a professor in the Department of Zoology, published a case study documenting the collaboration of librarian and subject researcher on a specific research project (Tennant and Miyamoto, 2008). It provided a unique insight into the research process from the librarian and subject faculty perspectives, showed the nature of collaboration between them, and documented the contribution of the embedded librarian to the research outcome.

A 2009 update on the status of the University of Florida program documented both successes and challenges. There has been significant staff turnover, and vacant positions have been eliminated in response to deep budget reductions. However, it appears that highly embedded librarians remain in place in some areas. The update discusses the struggles of the library organization over the varying degrees of embeddedness. The solution has been to define four *tiers* of service, which establish a framework for discussions with information user groups and library management. At tier one, the roles appear very similar to those of traditional academic liaison librarians discussed in Chapter 3—collection development, communication, and little more. At tier two, there are elements of relationship building and collaborating with subject faculty on teaching and other activities. At tiers three and four, the duties are much more in line with the examples of strong embedded relationships discussed in Chapters 1 and 3, including engagement in instruction and the research process (Ferree, et al., 2009).

The NIH established its informationist program and hired its first informationist in 2001. The library director laid the groundwork by meeting with senior managers of different units within the organization. Senior staff in the information user groups were enlisted to provide visible endorsement, mentor the new informationists, and enable them to learn about the work of their groups. Training plans were developed to ensure that the informationists would have the level of scientific knowledge needed to be effective members of the clinical and research teams. Over time, the responsibilities of informationists evolved from traditional library tasks to "critical appraisal and summarizing and synthesizing the literature, ... help with manuscript preparation, co-authoring articles and help with data analysis software" (Whitmore, Grefsheim, and Rankin, 2008,

p. 138). By 2008, the program had grown to 14 informationists, working with more than 40 information user groups in 16 different organizational units.

A preliminary analysis of evaluations conducted in 2004 and 2006 indicated that the presence of an informationist was associated with greater use of the available literature and better performance in finding answers to clinical and research questions. The evaluation summarized user reaction as "strong acceptance and uptake ... , growing demand for a wider variety of services, robust return on investment and unassailable satisfaction and loyalty ratings" (Whitmore, Grefsheim, and Rankin, 2008, p. 139).

Further documentation, published in 2010, noted that the NIH informationist program had increased to 15 staff members. Analyzing and comparing the 2004 and 2006 evaluations, the report found that collaboration with the informationists had become more widespread over time, as word of their ability and value spread among the researchers and clinicians. The presence of an informationist in a clinical or research group led to more-effective use of the literature and an increase in information user self-sufficiency in information retrieval. This doesn't mean that the informationists worked themselves out of a job, however. Instead, it was found that they took on a variety of technical information management and informatics-related tasks (Grefsheim, et al., 2010).

Perhaps the most prolific and influential contributors to the literature over a long period of sustained success are the management and staff of the Eskind Biomedical Library at Vanderbilt University. As noted earlier in this chapter, Giuse, then deputy director of the Eskind Biomedical Library, anticipated Davidoff and Florance with her 1997 call for clinical medical librarians to assume a coequal role with other healthcare professionals (Giuse, 1997).

Clinical medical librarianship was initiated at Eskind in 1996 with one librarian participating in rounds in the Medical Intensive Care Unit. The initial focus was on retrieving, filtering, and summarizing articles in response to questions that arose during the rounds. Initially, the clinical librarians did not charge for their work, so as not to be under pressure to demonstrate an immediate return on investment. The librarians recorded each clinical question they worked on in a database so that they could demonstrate the work that they had performed. In 1997, a 10-question opinion survey of the professionals with whom the clinical librarians collaborated found strong support for the librarians' work (Giuse, et al., 1998).

By 2004, the Eskind Biomedical Library had taken its model further. In 2001, the parent Medical Center implemented an electronic medical records system, called StarPanel. Recognizing the value of aligning its work with the new electronic workflow, the Library established in 2004 a capability to receive clinical questions via the secure messaging function of StarPanel. In response to these questions, a clinical librarian would prepare an information packet that retrieved, filtered, highlighted, and summarized the relevant literature. The final product would contain the librarian's summary, highlighted copies of all articles summarized, and a disclaimer noting that the summary was not intended to substitute for clinical judgment. The service was further expanded by incorporating links to standard guidelines into the StarPanel system and by extending the service to questions related to inpatient care practices. Yet none of these innovations replaced or eliminated the ongoing relationship of the informationist with other members of the clinical team. The authors noted that "librarians make regular 'drop-in' visits to the clinic to maintain visibility and continue to develop trust as well as collegiality with the clinicians" (Giuse, et al., 2005, p. 252).

An update published in 2010 (Giuse, Williams, and Giuse, 2010) demonstrated that the Eskind Biomedical Library continued to develop its informationist model. The update highlighted the following aspects of the program's integration and progression:

- Clinical Informatics Consult Service (CICS): Participate in rounds and provide evidence packets to clinical staff in response to specific patient-related needs.
- Patient Informatics Consult Service: Provide information packets to patients.
- StarPanel: Receive and respond to clinical questions using the Medical Center's electronic patient record system, thus integrating the information specialists into the mainstream of clinical workflow.
- Maintain and update order sets ("point-of-care actions ... usually grouped around a specific procedure [for example, asthma control]") within the electronic system (p. 221).
- Participate in the design and content creation for a new patient web portal, designed to "promote patients as more proactive partners in their care management and increase patient-provider communication" (p. 222).

Giuse, Williams, and Giuse concluded by observing that during the decade-plus history of clinical medical librarianship at Eskind Biomedical Library, the librarians have been "fully integrated … , thus allowing a true value-added scalable approach to the provision of evidence" and "an integral partnership of skills and competencies" (p. 222).

In other words, we might say they have become very highly embedded in the clinical enterprise.

Education and Training of Informationists

Education is an important, ongoing theme in the literature of embedded medical librarianship. Authors have held repeatedly that a substantial knowledge of medical science, in addition to a background in library and information science, is a requirement for success in the field. The emphasis on this point is much stronger in the medical library literature than in the literature of embedded librarianship in other sectors. Several articles have focused exclusively on the issue of education and training for clinical medical librarians and informationists.

Davidoff and Florance (2000) set the terms of this discussion in their manifesto, "The Informationist: A New Health Profession?" They called for informationists to have "a clear and solid understanding of both information science and the essentials of clinical work" (p. 997) and recognized the need for two tracks for the education of informationists: one for those who begin as librarians and the other for those who begin as clinical professionals.

Others soon elaborated on these recommendations. Detlefsen (2002) proposed five models for a comprehensive approach to the education of informationists:

- American Library Association accredited degree programs
- Training in universities and medical informatics centers not associated with American Library Association accredited programs
- Short courses and continuing education opportunities offered by academic health science centers
- Continuing education opportunities for librarianship, which might be offered by the Medical Library Association

- Distance education in both medical informatics and librarianship

Meanwhile, Hersh (2002), a faculty member at the Oregon Health and Science University, articulated a model of informationist training entirely outside librarianship. The model offered courses in medical informatics, health and medicine, computer science, and quantitative methods. Hersh argued that both library science and separate informatics educational programs were valid pathways for the development of informationists and could coexist in the healthcare field.

Vanderbilt University, continuing its leadership, developed an in-house training program for librarians without a background in biology, in order to equip them with bioinformatics knowledge (Lyon, et al., 2004). In the NIH informationist program (Robison, 2008), all have degrees in library and information science, while about half have prior education or experience in science or medicine, and all have worked in medical or science libraries. At NIH, the continuing education program includes the following elements:

- General courses in clinical research and biology
- Specialized courses in medicine and science relevant to the work of the group in which the informationist is embedded
- Learning by regular participation in lectures, conferences, rounds, and lab meetings

The American Medical Informatics Association website lists medical informatics programs both affiliated with schools of Library and Information Science and located in medical sciences institutes.

Best Practices

Beyond the issue of educational background, there are important questions regarding other competencies and organizational and management practices for initiating and sustaining the informationist or "information specialist in context" model.

Looking at the librarian's instructional role, Seago (2004) and Konieczny (2010) reached similar conclusions. In embedding information literacy instruction in the medical school curriculum, Seago emphasized the importance of having the support of the course director and incorporating a graded informatics assignment in one or more courses. Konieczny elaborated on the importance of the librarian's sharing with the subject instructor a clear understanding of their respective roles; having regular, reliable availability in course management systems; and meeting face-to-face with students if possible, or interacting with them via videoconference. The key is the quality of the relationships between librarian and instructor and between librarian and students.

Regarding relationship building and the development of trust in the clinical environment, Coldsmith and Schwing (2005) noted that success of an embedded clinical medical librarian in a residency program requires the commitment of all parties—the program director, the residency staff, and the librarian. The goal is that the residents "become comfortable" with librarians. In other words, they must develop a strong working relationship so that the residents will trust the librarians and rely on their information retrieval and analysis work products in making decisions. Brookman, et al. (2006) emphasized that trust is built over time through sustained visibility and ongoing commitment. They also noted that clinicians are eager for librarians to do more analysis—but only if the clinicians know and trust the librarians.

On the basis of an extensive review, Rankin, Grefsheim, and Canto (2008) recommended that to succeed, librarians must reverse a long-standing professional trend toward generalization and become specialists instead, with subject expertise relevant to the work of the information user groups in which they are embedded. Further, they found that an embedded relationship is necessary to "achieve credibility, acceptance, and sustainability," whereas an "impersonal information service provided at a distance" is less likely to achieve success (p. 195). They also reported that programs funded as part of the library's budget are more stable than those relying on funds from other sources.

Rankin, Grefsheim, and Canto (2008) also identified a range of enabling factors for embedded informationist programs. Enabling factors are organizational, programmatic, and service provider–related. Organizational factors include executive support and a supportive culture and environment. Programmatic factors include marketing; visibility; delivery of a high-quality, sophisticated work product; and evaluation or feedback. Service provider factors include characteristics such as a high level of professional competence and interpersonal skills to form strong, trusted working relationships. These required competencies are summarized in Figure 4.1.

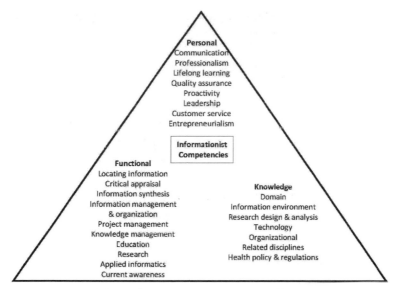

Figure 4.1   Informationist Competencies [Source: Rankin, J. A., Grefsheim, S. F., & Canto, C. C. (2008). The emerging informationist specialty: A systematic review of the literature. Journal of the Medical Library Association, 96(3), 199. Used by permission.]

The experience of the Arizona Health Sciences Library illustrates the application of these practices. Seizing the opportunity created by construction of a new multidisciplinary research building, the library director won senior administrator support to provide space for embedded librarians. When the building opened, four librarians, including several with prior specialized subject education, were placed in it part-time. They continued to be funded by the library budget. Their former duties at the main library reference desk were covered by merging the reference and circulation desks and training paraprofessional employees to handle most types of requests.

Within a year, the library deployed an additional librarian to work with the College of Pharmacy and extended the program to the College of Nursing. Librarians were regular attendees at faculty meetings. Librarians were being written into grant applications, embedded information literacy instruction was up 40 percent, and librarians had come to be viewed as "partners who can contribute significantly to the mission of the colleges and the university" (Freiburger and Kramer, 2009, p. 141).

In reviewing the program's success, Freiburger and Kramer echoed the factors highlighted by Rankin, et al.:

- Organizational support: Information user-group commitment in the form of support from a dean or associate dean of each college
- Programmatic support: Sustained effort on the part of library management, with provision of equipment, freeing embedded librarians from other duties, and ongoing promotion through visits to faculty meetings and class sessions, special events, and other outreach efforts
- Service provider skills: The combination of domain education, information competencies, and interpersonal skills of the embedded librarians

Evaluations of Clinical Medical Librarianship

The literature on embedded librarianship in the health sciences is distinguished by its emphasis on evaluation. From the early days of clinical medical librarianship to the present, medical librarians have recognized the need to demonstrate that the embedded librarian can and does have a real impact on the behavior of clinical staff, the use of the medical literature, and ultimately the quality of medical care.

Adopting the methodology of the medical field, Marshall and Neufeld (1981) performed a randomized trial field experiment, assigning four healthcare teams to the study group and four to a control group. A clinical librarian was assigned to each team in the study group and worked with the team for 6 months. At that time, interviews were conducted with the members of all eight groups, and a second round of interviews was conducted 3 months later.

Marshall and Neufeld also collected data about the work of the clinical librarians. They found that the librarians interacted with virtually everyone in the clinical environment. They received almost 600 requests: 24 percent from patients, 40 percent from physicians, 21 percent from allied health professionals, and 15 percent from nurses. Of the 444 searches done for health professionals (not patients), more than 25 percent (113) were information needs recognized by the clinical librarians—not direct requests made by the healthcare team. In other words, the librarians often recognized needs not articulated by the other members of the team.

Additional data showed that the study group members made much greater use of library resources overall than the control group members did. For example, the study groups accounted for more than 15 times the number of online search requests by the control groups. This difference in library use was found to persist, but at lower levels, after the clinical librarians were withdrawn (Marshall and Neufeld, 1981).

Marshall and Neufeld also found that comments made in the interviews showed the impact and value of the clinical librarians:

- Some 70 percent of the study group members found the librarian "very helpful."
- Many staff, especially nurses and allied health professionals, said they used library services for the first time after the clinical librarian program began.
- Physicians noted that they became aware of many questions that were raised during rounds but not followed up.
- And 83 percent of study group members said that the librarian had provided useful information that they would not have found otherwise.

Two-thirds of the study group members said that their information-seeking habits were changed by their experience with the clinical librarians. Additional responses showed that library resources became their highest-rated information sources, superseding colleagues and their own books and journals overall. The authors conclude that "clinical librarians serving health professionals, patients, and families can be successful" and "there are significant changes in information-seeking patterns among health professionals who receive the services of a clinical librarian" (p. 416).

Kay Cimpl Wagner (formerly Kay Cimpl) has done the field a great service by completing two reviews of the literature almost 20 years apart. Her first review (Cimpl, 1985) summarized eight programs, all at university medical centers in North America. She noted a wide range of documented benefits, including enhanced patient care, educational benefits for medical students and healthcare teams, time savings, greater exposure to the literature, and greater information sharing among colleagues.

Cimpl (1985) also noted a few objections. Some can be attributed to lack of skill and knowledge on the part of the medical librarian—misunderstanding of questions and delivery of unsolicited, irrelevant information.

In one case, the service was discontinued because it seemed to be competing with traditional library reference service. She also found cost to be a major obstacle. Most of the programs she reviewed were funded by the library, not by the clinical programs. Where the costs were deemed prohibitive, she suggested that the calculation failed to take into account the various benefits of the program to the clinical staff or did not involve a comprehensive cost-effectiveness evaluation.

Kay Cimpl Wagner's second review, co-authored with Gary Byrd (2004), identified 35 papers that reported a formal evaluation, by either quantitative or qualitative methods. It included papers from Nigeria and the U.K., in addition to Canada and the U.S. Wagner and Byrd noted that only four of the 35 studies used before-and-after evaluation, or comparison control groups. In the end, their detailed analysis found equivocal conclusions:

> There is some relatively strong evidence that these programs have been well accepted and liked by most of the targeted clinicians and students served. However, the total amount of such evidence is not great, most of it is descriptive rather than comparative or analytically qualitative, and it does not rise to the level of the "best evidence" called for to support evidence-based medicine or librarianship. (pp. 30–31)

Medical librarians have continued to study and report the value of their embedded librarianship programs. A review by Weightman and Williamson (2005) examined the reported impacts of both traditional library services and clinical librarians on healthcare. Analyzing 28 studies, the authors found evidence that both traditional library services and clinical medical librarians have an impact on healthcare. "There is also evidence, notably from the clinical librarian studies, of time savings to healthcare professionals and cost-benefits" (p. 17). However, they qualified their findings with concerns over the size and quality of the research studies.

Among the more recent evaluations of embedded librarianship in medical settings, Schwing and Coldsmith (2005) found that, after maintaining their program for 2 years, 58 percent of the hospital residents surveyed said that the answers provided by the librarian influenced patient care "much" or "a great deal" (p. 36). However, only 40 percent said that they asked for the librarian's help "frequently."

In a British study, Brookman, et al. (2006) evaluated specific information searches that the clinical librarians conducted. The most common reason for requesting a search was patient care, and 50 percent of these searches resulted in a change in practice. Similarly, searches conducted for other purposes were highly rated, and overall, 85 percent of searches received a rating of 4 or 5 on a 5-point scale (with 5 being the most positive rating).

A team at Vanderbilt University conducted a randomized trial of its CICS in the intensive care unit during 19 months spanning 2004 to 2006 (Mulvaney, et al., 2008). During this period, all requests to the clinical informationists were randomly assigned to either receive a response or not. (Clinicians were able to opt out of the randomization process, and about 10 percent of the cases in the study were "opt-outs.") The Vanderbilt team studied results of more than 200 requests for information and found that the CICS had a statistically significant, positive impact on the use of evidence in diagnosis, care, and treatment. Furthermore, clinicians who requested information from the CICS were also more likely to perform searches themselves, suggesting a synergistic effect between the role of the embedded informationist and information seeking by the clinical staff.

What Lies Ahead

Throughout its development, embedded librarians in the health sciences have exemplified traits in common with embedded librarians in other sectors: a strong emphasis on building relationships with other medical professionals, becoming knowledgeable in the subject domain, and performing at a high level of sophistication and skill to add value to the mission of the parent organization. Health sciences librarians have recognized the importance of continuous change since the early days of the development of their clinical role, and the process of change continues today.

The idea that the medical library not only should change, but must change, has become a fixture in predictions about the role of libraries and librarians in healthcare. Already in 1995, Nina Matheson, director emerita of the Welch Medical Library at Johns Hopkins University, predicted that "[t]he time is coming ... when libraries must choose between owning traditional resources and making them available; developing and owning new digital knowledge resources and making them accessible; or being an organization that knows where knowledge is and teaches how to mine it" (pp. 4–5). Just 2 years later, Giuse (1997) sharpened the point by adding, "We have *no choice* but to migrate into the clinical setting; to avoid doing so is to deny our future in the information age" (p. 437; italics in the original).

A few years later, Donald Lindberg and Betsy Humphreys (2005), director and deputy director, respectively, of the National Library of Medicine, laid out their own vision of the future in the *New England Journal of Medicine*. Avoiding Matheson's stark choice, they offered inferences for the year 2015:

> More librarians and information specialists are deployed "in context" outside the library to improve quality, to reduce the risks associated with inefficient or incomplete retrieval of the available evidence, and to do community outreach. Many librarians have advanced training in both subject-matter disciplines and information science. It is common to find librarians working as part of health care teams, writing grant proposals, serving on institutional review boards, working as bioinformatics database specialists within science departments, serving as faculty members in evidence-based medicine courses, and being involved in multilingual health-literacy programs and community partnerships. (para. 9)

In other words, embedded librarianship is a key element of their vision.

Circling back to Johns Hopkins, in 2010, Nancy Roderer, successor to Matheson as director of the Welch Medical Library, articulated a specific, near-term plan that fulfills Matheson's vision. In accord with a clinician's observation that "if the materials are going to be coming to me, then the librarians should too" (Kho, 2011, p. 1), the Welch Medical Library will distribute its librarians to the clinical and research teams as embedded informationists and reuse its building for other than traditional library purposes (Kolowich, 2010).

It's clear that some 40 years after the first medical librarian joined clinicians on their rounds, embedded librarianship is not just alive and well, but a key element of the future of healthcare information.

Summary

This chapter showed how embedded librarianship in the healthcare field arose in the 1970s to meet a need. That need was to better utilize evidence from the literature in the diagnosis and treatment of disease and in the care of patients. Initial programs had some success, and early studies were able to document the fact that the programs resulted in more-extensive use of literature.

Along the way, the clinical medical librarians recognized that the problem was greater than simple access to articles—it also involved having the time to read the literature and synthesize the results. Accordingly, leaders in the field called for a new role, initially called *informationist* and later sometimes *information specialist in context*—a professional with both expertise in information retrieval and a sophisticated understanding of the clinical environment, able to identify, retrieve, read, and summarize the literature in order to provide direct input into clinical questions and to teach health sciences students how to use the available knowledge effectively for themselves. These services have become well established in many institutions, although we don't know how many, as there is no comprehensive census.

Meanwhile, other developments created an even greater need for embedded medical librarians. Paradoxically, as more and more health science literature became available in digital form anytime, anywhere, through mobile communication devices, the sheer increase in its volume and the proliferation of interfaces, tools, and digital library resources increased the complexity of the research process. Greater emphasis was placed on information literacy skills, and at the same time the value of the traditional medical library with its emphasis on collecting paper copies of information resources was called into question.

References

American Medical Informatics Association. n.d. Academic informatics programs. Available from www.amia.org/education/programs-and-courses. (Accessed April 4, 2012.)

Brookman, A., A. Lovell, F. Henwood, and J. Lehmann. 2006. What do clinicians want from us? An evaluation of Brighton and Sussex University Hospitals NHS Trust Clinical Librarian Service and its implications for developing future working patterns. *Health Information and Libraries Journal* 23 (December): 10–21.

Cimpl, K. 1985. Clinical medical librarianship: A review of the literature. *Bulletin of the Medical Library Association* 73 (1): 21–28.

Coumou, H. C. H., and F. J. Meijman. 2006. How do primary care physicians seek answers to clinical questions. *Journal of the Medical Library Association* 94 (1): 55–60.

Cousins, J., and K. Perris. 2009. Supporting research at the faculty of medicine: The development of Imperial College London's Medicine Information Literacy Group. *Journal of Information Literacy* 3 (1): 60–67.

Davidoff, F., and V. Florance. 2000. The informationist: A new health profession? *Annals of Internal Medicine* 132 (12): 996–998.

Detlefsen, E. G. 2002. The education of informationists, from the perspective of a library and information sciences educator. *Journal of the American Medical Library Association* 90 (1): 59–67.

Dryer, B. V. 1962. Lifetime learning for physicians: Principles, practices, proposals. *Journal of Medical Education* 37 (6): 1–134.

Ferree, N., N. Schaefer, L. C. Butson, and M. R. Tennant. 2009. Liaison librarian tiers: Levels of service. *Journal of the Medical Library Association* 97 (2): 145–148.

Flynn, M. G., and C. McGuinness. 2011. Hospital clinicians' information behaviour and attitude towards the 'clinical informationist': An Irish survey. *Health Information and Libraries Journal* 28 (1): 23–32.

Freiburger, G., and S. Kramer. 2009. Embedded librarians: One library's model for decentralized service. *Journal of the Medical Library Association* 97 (2): 139–142.

Giuse, N. B. 1997. Advancing the practice of clinical medical librarianship. *Bulletin of the Medical Library Association* 85 (4): 437–438.

Giuse, N. B., A. M. Williams, and D. A. Giuse. 2010. Integrating best evidence into patient care: A process facilitated by a seamless integration with informatics tools. *Journal of the Medical Library Association* 98 (3): 220–222.

Giuse, N. B., S. R. Kafantaris, M. D. Miller, K. S. Wilder, S. L. Martin, N. A. Sathe, and J. D. Campbell. 1998. Clinical medical librarianship: The Vanderbilt experience. *Bulletin of the Medical Library Association* 86 (3): 412–416.

Giuse, N. B., T. Y. Koonce, R. N. Jerome, M. Cahall, N. A. Sathe, and A. Williams. 2005. Evolution of a mature clinical informationist model. *Journal of the American Medical Informatics Association* 12 (3): 249–255.

Grefsheim, S. F., S. C. Whitmore, B. A. Rapp, J. A. Rankin, R. R. Robison, and C. C. Canto. 2010. The informationist: Building evidence for an emerging health profession. *Journal of the Medical Library Association* 98 (2): 147–156.

Guillot, L., B. Stahr, and B. J. Meeker. 2010. Nursing faculty collaborate with embedded librarians to serve online graduate students in a consortium setting. *Journal of Library and Information Services in Distance Learning* 1 (1/2): 53–62.

Hersh, W. 2002. Medical informatics education: An alternative pathway for training informationists. *Journal of the Medical Information Association* 90 (1): 76–79.

Kates, J. 1978. What's obstetrics coming to? Ask the women at McMaster: At McMaster University, giving birth is a remarkable experience. *Globe and Mail, Canada*, September 13.

Kho, N. D. 2011. Embedded librarianship: Building relational roles. *Information Today* 28 (3): 1–36.

Kolowich, S. 2010. Embedded librarians: Johns Hopkins ahead of curve. *USA Today*, June 9. Available from www.usatoday.com/news/education/2010-06-09-IHE-embedded-librarians-Johns-Hopkins09_ST_N.htm. (Accessed April 4, 2012.)

Konieczny, A. 2010. Experiences as an embedded librarian in online courses. *Medical Reference Services Quarterly* 29 (1): 47–57.

Lindberg, D. A. B., and B. L. Humphreys. 2005. 2015—the future of medical libraries. *New England Journal of Medicine* 325 (11): 1067–1070.

Lyon, J., N. B. Giuse, A. Williams, T. Y. Koonce, and R. Walden. 2004. A model for training the new bioinformationist. *Journal of the Medical Library Association* 92 (2): 188–195.

Marshall, J. G., and V. R. Neufeld. 1981. A randomized trial of librarian educational participation in clinical settings. *Journal of Medical Education* 56: 409–416.

Matheson, N. W. 1995. The idea of the library in the twenty-first century. *Bulletin of the Medical Library Association* 83 (1): 1–7.

Mulvaney, S. A., L. Bickman, N. B. Giuse, E. W. Lambert, N. A. Sathe, and R. N. Jerome. 2008. A randomized effectiveness trial of a clinical informatics consult service: Impact on evidence-based decision-making and knowledge implementation. *Journal of the American Medical Informatics Association* 15 (2): 201–211.

Perry, G. J., and M. R. Kronenfeld. 2005. Evidence-based practice: A new paradigm brings new opportunities for health sciences librarians. *Medical Reference Services Quarterly* 24 (4): 1–16.

Plutchak, T. S. 2000. Informationists and librarians. *Bulletin of the Medical Library Association* 88 (4): 391–392.

Rankin, J. A., S. F. Grefsheim, and C. C. Canto. 2008. The emerging informationist specialty: A systematic review of the literature. *Journal of the Medical Library Association* 96 (3): 194–206.

Robison, R. R. 2008. Informationist education. *Medical Reference Services Quarterly* 27 (3): 339–347.

Roseman, E. 1978. The consumer game: Some hospitals listening to patients' complaints. *Globe and Mail, Canada*, July 31.

Schwing, L. J., and E. E. Coldsmith. 2005. Librarians as hidden gems in a clinical team. *Medical Reference Services Quarterly* 24 (1): 29–39.

Seago, B. L. 2004. School of medicine CBIL librarian: An educational informationist model. *Reference Services Review* 32 (1): 35–39.

Shipman, J. P., D. J. Cunningham, R. Holst, and L. A. Watson. 2002. The informationist conference: Report. *Journal of the Medical Librarians Association* 90 (4): 458–464.

Tennant, M. R., and M. M. Miyamoto. 2008. The role of the medical librarian in the basic biological sciences: A case study in virology and evolution. *Journal of the Medical Library Association* 96 (4): 290–298.

Tennant, M. R., L. C. Butson, M. E. Rezeau, P. J. Tucker, M. E. Boyle, and G. Clayton. 2001. Customizing for clients: Developing a library liaison program from need to plan. *Bulletin of the Medical Library Association* 89 (1): 8–20.

Tennant, M. R., T. T. Cataldo, P. Sherwill-Navarro, and R. Jesano. 2006. Evaluation of a liaison librarian program: Client and liaison perspectives. *Journal of the Medical Library Association* 94 (4): 402–409.

Tod, A. M., B. Bond, N. Leonard, I. J. Gilsen, and S. Palfreyman. 2007. Exploring the contribution of the clinical librarian to facilitating evidence-based nursing. *Journal of Clinical Nursing* 16 (4): 621–629.

Wagner, K. C., and G. D. Byrd. 2004. Evaluating the effectiveness of clinical medical librarian programs: A systematic review of the literature. *Journal of the Medical Library Association* 92 (1): 14–33.

Weightman, A. L., and J. M. Williamson. 2005. The value and impact of information provided through library services for patient care: A systematic review. *Health Information and Libraries Journal* 22: 4–25.

Whitmore, S. C., S. F. Grefsheim, and J. A. Rankin. 2008. Informationist programme in support of biomedical research: A programme description and preliminary findings of an evaluation. *Health Information and Libraries Journal* 25: 135–141.

Chapter 5

Embedded Librarians in Corporations, Nonprofits, and Government

The literature on embedded librarianship in corporations, nonprofits, and government agencies is not as extensive as the literature pertaining to higher education; nor is it as systematic and analytical as that related to health sciences and healthcare. A contributed paper for the Special Libraries Association (SLA) noted the paucity of published examples (Shumaker and Tyler, 2007). The problem didn't seem to stem from a failure of librarians in these organizations to adopt the embedded model, however. The paper reported on a survey, which was conducted with a convenience sample of subscribers to several professional email lists, found that more than 80 percent of those listing an affiliation by organization type were in a for-profit (43 percent), nonprofit (21 percent) or government (20 percent) entity. Only 17 percent of respondents identified themselves as working in an institution of higher education.

A subsequent survey by Shumaker and Talley (2009) found similar results. This survey, administered to a random sample of SLA members, once again found that 43 percent of embedded respondents reported working in the for-profit sector, while 16 percent were in government and 11 percent in not-for-profit organizations. The percentage of respondents in higher education was somewhat higher than in the earlier survey, at 28 percent.

Regardless of actual adoption, the available information about patterns of embedded librarianship in this sector is far sparser than in the other sectors. This chapter explores the origins of embedded librarianship in corporations, nonprofits, and government and mines the recent literature for indications of the nature of embedded librarians' work, how their contributions are evaluated, organizational patterns, the overall health of the embedded model in this sector, and the outlook for the future.

Origins

It would be strange indeed if librarians in the corporate sector had not adopted the embedded model. As we saw in Chapter 1, Tom Davenport and Larry Prusak (1993) issued their clarion call to "Blow Up the Corporate Library" almost 20 years ago. By then, the weaknesses of the traditional corporate library were clear. Libraries had become just-in-case warehouses of mostly textual published material. In some corporations, the warehouse of texts was augmented by a warehouse of experts—subject specialists who could respond to specific questions. Meanwhile, librarians missed opportunities to integrate their resources with the computer-based quantitative internal performance data generated by the new generation of management information specialists. Mistakenly, the librarians concentrated on achieving functional efficiency in library operations, not strategic value. They thus failed to deliver visible contributions, in an environment becoming increasingly performance- and measurement-oriented.

Davenport and Prusak (1993) offered a concrete course correction for corporate librarians. They advocated that "librarians, or rather information managers, must view themselves not as warehouse custodians, or even as providers of centralized expertise, but rather as overseers of a multi-media network" (p. 408). They concluded with an 8-point plan. The first two are foundations for the embedded model:

1. "Get out of the library, and into the business.
2. "Actively assess who needs information, and who has it—then help them to connect" (p. 412).

Also in 1993, Michel Bauwens, a Belgian corporate librarian, published a personal account that we can read, with 20/20 hindsight, as a prophecy of two decades of corporate librarianship. He recounted the reduction of the Business Intelligence Unit from 15 employees to one—himself. He envisioned the new corporate librarian as being "in the middle of a concentric circle of cyberspace (i.e., the electronic information space or ocean" (para. 6). He advocated that the corporation that takes information seriously should create "a network of cybrarians (i.e., librarians able to navigate in 'cyberspace'), strategically located throughout the company" (para. 10). He foresaw that "[t]hese well-trained, IT literate individuals will be integrated into management teams" (para. 11).

In the ensuing years, as the surveys cited at the beginning of this chapter indicate, corporate librarians began to adopt new models that approximated the visions of Davenport, Prusak, and Bauwens. That model conforms to embedded librarianship. Shumaker and Tyler (2007) found little literature to document this evolution, but change was happening, although corporate librarians didn't write about it very much.

The evolution of embedded librarianship was often confused with the internet revolution and the shift to virtual or digital library services and collections. In a 2002 article, "A Traditional Library Goes Virtual," Stephanie Boyd discussed the creation of a library call center to take reference questions quickly and efficiently, and inserted the following observation, almost as an aside:

> To date, only a small percentage of requests come in via our call center, since the majority of our clients choose to direct their questions to a researcher they know. We have encouraged this close relationship between our researchers and their clients, and in fact we aim to develop subject matter expertise within our team for the different client groups. (p. 44)

Also in 2002, Kathy Dempsey, a library marketing specialist, began to supply the ingredient of relationship building, but only in a very limited way. Among her recommended tactics to raise the visibility of librarians: "Make friends," "Become personal researchers" (p. 78), and hold face-to-face meetings with potential information users to explain capabilities and offer services.

By 2004, the first attempt to assess the success of embedded librarianship was published, although the term *embedded* wasn't used. "The New Information Professional," an article in *Information Outlook*, reported the results of a project funded by SLA in 2002. The study focused on newspaper publishers. It compared the recognition accorded to librarians embedded in reporting teams with the recognition accorded to librarians working in traditionally organized, centralized libraries. The researcher, Deborah Barreau, concluded that "organizations with [a] researcher assigned to editorial teams acknowledged contributions more often, but the correlation is slight and the results are inconclusive" (Barreau, 2004, p. 32).

The inconclusive results of Barreau's investigation notwithstanding, descriptions of embedded librarianship began to pick up a bit in the succeeding years. The annual SLA conferences regularly featured presentations on the subject, beginning in 2005 with a panel discussion. A presentation by John Peverley of Bain & Company, titled "Embedding

Researchers in Case Teams: The Bain & Company Experience," described how Bain's larger offices had projects large enough to require the services of researchers on case teams. Those researchers would develop expertise, attend consultant staffing calls, and interact in real time with customers. Each researcher was considered an integral part of the small working groups, acting as a "trusted advisor" to the team (Peverley, 2005). The next year, Shumaker discussed management of embedded library services at the MITRE Corp. in a presentation entitled "Moving to Client-Embedded Services: Building and Sustaining Embedded Information Services" (Shumaker, 2006). Also in 2006, Moore published a description of his experiences as an embedded librarian at MITRE (Moore, 2006). The SLA presentation by Shumaker and Tyler in 2007 represented the first attempt to describe the characteristics and extent of embedded librarianship in corporations, as well as other types of organizations. A steady trickle of publications about embedded librarianship in corporations, nonprofits, and government agencies continues. Even though librarians in this sector still are not publishing very much, some evidence exists from which to infer roles, functions, and other characteristics of embedded librarianship.

Roles and Functions

Successful embedded librarians provide sophisticated contributions to the teams they work with. However, the available evidence indicates that the nature of the work varies among different organizational sectors. Academic librarians focus on embedded instruction, contributing to the pedagogical mission of their institutions. The emphasis in the health sciences community is on research—providing evidence from the literature to help clinicians make decisions about patient treatment and care. Other themes also surface, such as embedded instruction, especially in teaching hospitals and other academic institutions, and an emerging role in managing the large volumes of data generated by biomedical research projects.

The corporate and government sector is clearly different from the academic sector. The *Models of Embedded Librarianship* research project, funded by the SLA, found that corporate and government embedded librarians were much more likely than librarians in other types of organizations to perform a number of research and information delivery tasks, including the following:

- Competitive intelligence
- Evaluating, synthesizing, and summarizing the literature
- Current awareness and news alerting
- Interlibrary loan and document delivery (Shumaker, 2011a)

Similarly, the project found that in the corporate and government sectors, embedded librarians were more likely than in other sectors to participate in the management and analysis of internal knowledge and information. The kinds of tasks in which the study found differences included structured database development and management, information architecture, and management of document repositories.

The available descriptions of embedded librarians' work in the corporate sector reinforce this analysis. Moore (2006) described his "service portfolio" in these terms:

- Stewarding content—tagging and linking
- Providing news alerts
- Capturing knowledge
- Researching

Several articles have documented the research role of embedded librarians at Ziba Design, a design consulting firm. Reece Dano, one of Ziba's embedded librarians, described his primary role as "secondary research," which includes identifying consumer and market trends, analyzing popular sentiment, and helping to "generate hypotheses about consumers by analyzing relevant secondary market and consumer research" (Spencer, 2009, p. 28). In a subsequent article, Dano and his colleague Gretchen McNeely (2011) asserted that for an embedded librarian, "discovering information gaps is the meat of every project;" to do this entails "… auditing and assessing available information … as well as determining how to retrieve information not currently at hand" (p. 3).

Jill Stover Heinze (2010) emphasized the importance of her research skills and ability to monitor the external environment—skills complementary to the skills of the marketing communications group in which she was embedded. The pairing of her research with their marketing knowledge led to opportunities such as co-authoring a corporate white paper and industry articles on legislative impacts that demonstrated the firm's thought leadership position among peers and potential clients.

At an unnamed law firm, the range of work done by embedded librarians included research and analysis for the firm's marketing department and its mergers and acquisitions practice. For its company representation practice, the embedded librarians began by stewarding an intranet-based repository related to regulatory filings. They were then called on for research tasks as their subject domain knowledge grew (Shumaker and Talley, 2009). When Shumaker revisited the firm in 2011, he found further examples of content and repository management combined with research and analysis. For a time, an embedded librarian had been assigned to work with another staff member to create a news- and issue-tracking database for the firm's benefits and compensation practice group (Shumaker, 2011b).

The pattern of combining research and analysis with content and knowledge management has a great appeal. Many corporate and government settings emphasize the ability to make well-informed decisions and take action in a timely and effective manner—not on the skills of information retrieval and management. Information expertise, like expertise in other areas, is valued when it is clearly linked to effective decision making and timely action. Smart marketers, attorneys, engineers, and other professionals are willing to delegate information-related tasks to embedded librarians, just as they delegate other tasks, when they see that delegating is the most effective way to accomplish their objectives. By taking ownership of the full range of information-related tasks, the librarian in turn becomes the knowledge expert on the team. And, as the knowledge expert, the librarian is positioned to fulfill a key aspect of the vision that Bauwens (1993) advanced in his Cybrarians Manifesto.

Bauwens (1993) advocated that cybrarians think of themselves not as traditional intermediaries, but as network nodes in three dimensions: "first of all amongst each other, second with the teams [with which they are embedded], third to a network of outside information providers (other cybrarians and experts on the internet, information brokers)" (para. 10). Until now, the focus of this book has really been on the second of these three dimensions, the relationship of the embedded librarian with the other members of the team. Through the research and analysis function, the librarian also establishes the third network: relationships with the network of experts, vendors, and information brokers, as well as expertise in using document and information resources of all kinds. Finally, as the information expert on the team, the embedded librarian has a natural affinity with other embedded information experts. By cultivating their own network, embedded librarians not only develop common methods to address needs and solve problems they share; they can also facilitate the sharing of knowledge across the organization. In recognition of this benefit, leading information services in corporations are establishing formal mechanisms to build and sustain these networks. One such initiative has taken place at the MITRE Corp., where "clusters" of embedded librarians "serve as vehicles for mentoring and sharing expertise, enhancing collaboration, identifying and connecting [cross-organizational] projects, and linking research and knowledge management needs across the corporation" (Trimble, 2010, p. 24). This realizes Bauwens's vision of embedded librarians networking with each other.

Evaluation

The preceding two chapters demonstrated that evaluation of the embedded librarian's contribution is very important in both the higher education and the medical settings. Academic librarians are working to establish formal learning goals related to information literacy and exploring ways to connect embedded instruction to student academic success. Medical librarians have conducted a variety of studies, even including at least one controlled, randomized trial, to assess the value of clinical medical librarians and informationists to healthcare practice and patient outcomes.

The corporate and government sectors are different. Over the years, specialized librarians and information professionals in these sectors have repeatedly been exhorted to measure their value in return on investment, time saved, costs saved, and similar measures. Barreau's research contributed to this approach. Kaplan and Norton's Balanced Scorecard has been recommended as a framework for developing goals and measuring outcomes (Matthews, 2003; Matarazzo and Pearlstein, 2007). However, in the reports from practitioners of embedded librarianship in this sector, formal evaluation plays a very limited role.

Evaluation practices were part of the discussions in two separate research visits, in 2009 and 2011, at a large, international law firm (Shumaker and Talley, 2009; Shumaker, 2011b). In the first visit, only librarians and the library manager (the chief library and records officer of the firm) were interviewed. The researchers reported the following:

> The Chief noted that the firm does not require ROI [return on investment] or other success measurements, maintenance of

> statistics or other data to justify the continuation of the pro-
> grams. Accordingly, there are no formal evaluations of the
> programs. The Chief does collect and acknowledge kudos
> received for work well done. Growth in the demand for ser-
> vices within the programs and demand for new programs are
> proof of success. (Shumaker and Talley, 2009, p. B-3)

In the second visit, managers of information user groups were interviewed, in addition to the embedded librarians and the chief library and
records officer. The situation had not changed. Feedback was still informal and anecdotal. The information user-group managers reinforced the
previous findings. They felt that they were in a position to assess the
nature of the librarians' contributions firsthand. They had high praise for
the librarians' expertise and contributions to the work. They felt that if
there were ever a need to address a performance problem or the value of
the librarians' work, they could approach the chief library and records
officer directly and be sure of an effective response. Both noted that the
management culture of the firm encouraged informal collaboration
among executives, rather than formal reporting mechanisms, and that the
management and evaluation of embedded librarians was consistent with
this culture. One summed up her assessment of librarians' value by saying
that the librarian "makes everybody do such a better job" (p. 25).

Echoing that assessment, Jill Stover Heinze commented that one of her
company's top executives refers to her as "the person who helps make
everyone in the company smarter" (Shumaker and Strand, 2009, p. 42). In
describing her role at Affinion Loyalty Group, she highlighted the importance of collaboration, relationships, and informal interactions in making
awareness of her skills and her value immediately apparent to her colleagues and company executives (Heinze, 2010).

At a large, privately held multinational corporation, the approach to
evaluating embedded librarians is somewhat more formal (Shumaker,
2011b). Here, mid-level managers of groups who engage embedded librarians pay an annual fee from their budget. The central InfoCenter operation in turn manages and coordinates the network of librarians, in a way
that is somewhat similar to that of the MITRE Corp. and to Michel
Bauwens's vision. Within the InfoCenter there are two directors who function as key management relationship managers. One of their practices is
to hold "regular, usually semi-annual, meetings with key business unit
heads. These meetings include discussion of business unit plans and

related information needs; a review of information services and perform-ance; and establishing the funding allocation from the business unit to the InfoCenter" (p. 36). Feedback received at these meetings, as well as other comments received from information users, is incorporated in the per-formance reviews of embedded librarians. The corporation also uses a 360-degree performance review process, and information users are invited to contribute to these performance reviews. This corporation does not try to calculate a formal, quantitative measure of the value of embed-ded librarians' work, but it does have a systematic way of incorporating information user feedback in individual performance reviews, as well as in library management decisions.

Organizational Patterns

Another challenge of assessing embedded librarianship in this sector is that the embedded librarians don't always work in a library or information services unit. Sometimes they are directly employed by information user groups, whether or not an identifiable library organization exists. Heinze (2010) was hired as a solo research analyst in the marketing department at her firm. In the U.S. government, there are agencies in which librarians are embedded in specific offices to perform research, analysis, and knowl-edge management functions independent of the agency's library. In some cases they are categorized as librarians, but in others they may be labeled program analysts, information specialists, intelligence analysts, or infor-mation technology staff. This phenomenon is difficult to quantify, and there is no known comprehensive assessment of it.

Challenges and Opportunities

To assess the outlook for the future of the embedded model in these organizations, it helps to pull in literature from a related, yet quite differ-ent, object of study: the literature of corporate library closings.

Similar to the perception that the embedded librarianship model is growing, the perception that there is a trend toward the closure of special-ized libraries, especially in the for-profit sector, has been prevalent in the literature in the first decade of the 21st century. Since no comprehensive documentation exists, it's difficult to understand both trends fully. Yet two researchers, James Matarazzo and Toby Pearlstein, have attempted an analysis. Their insights are also instructive in considering the prospects for embedded librarianship.

Matarazzo and Pearlstein published a series of articles during 2009 and 2010 in *Searcher* magazine under the heading "Survival Lessons for Libraries." Two of the articles documented actual experiences in the closure of libraries, in the U.S. Environmental Protection Agency and in American newspaper libraries (Pearlstein and Matarazzo, 2009b; Matarazzo and Pearlstein, 2010). Others dealt with questions of outsourcing (Pearlstein and Matarazzo, 2009a; Pearlstein and Matarazzo, 2009b) and the use of scenario planning as a strategic management tool for librarians (Matarazzo and Pearlstein, 2009).

Throughout the series, the authors referred to a predictive model of library closures, which associates the threat with five conditions:

- Decision made by senior management, without consulting those who used the library
- Library experiencing a reduction in the number of its users
- The availability of outside resources to substitute for the library
- A lack of library evaluation
- Evidence of a financial crisis in the parent organization

In their discussion of outsourcing, the authors offered three recommendations to corporate library managers:

- Be prepared to participate in outsourcing decisions; be informed and communicate your insights.
- Reinforce the library's alignment with the parent organization's goals.
- "Have/put processes in place to minimize need for new head count [additional staffing]" (Pearlstein and Matarazzo, 2009a, p. 37).

A sidebar (Montgomery, 2010) to the final article in the series offered three questions that librarians and library managers should ask themselves regularly:

- What are my strengths?

- What do I need to learn as our business changes?
- How am I connected to business development? (p. 47)

The series barely mentioned embedded librarianship. It is the thesis of this book, and this chapter in particular, that the conditions for successful embedded librarianship are different from Matarazzo and Pearlstein's scenario and that embedded librarianship offers a very different definition and set of recommendations for success.

In terms of the opportunities for success, Matarazzo and Pearlstein (2010) pointed out that success is never guaranteed. As they put it, "In some instances, no matter how good you are, no matter how well aligned with your parent organization, no matter how much those with the purse strings appreciate what a library can do for their business, if the whole enterprise is going under, there is nothing to do but package yourself for another opportunity" (p. 49). There's also nothing you can do to inoculate yourself against bad management decisions. Bad decisions are made even in successful companies, and librarians can end up on the wrong end of some of them.

But, more to the point of the outlook for embedded librarianship, the successful embedded librarian is one who takes a fundamentally different viewpoint from the library manager trying to defend a library unit. The embedded librarian's concern is the success of the team, and the concern of the manager of a group of embedded librarians is on the achievement of corporate goals (in accord with the second of Matarazzo and Pearlstein's three recommendations).

Furthermore, the successful embedded librarian has a broad view of the librarian's role. It is not to provide just expert research service, or information literacy instruction, or the management of internal content. The embedded librarian's role is to help the team use information most effectively in its operations, and the manager's role is to help the organization optimize its use of information—by the most appropriate means available. That means that embedded librarians are constantly trying to work themselves out of a job. It also means that they are change leaders, not change followers. And it means that they are in a position to experience sustained success.

If the preceding seems a bit farfetched—a rhetorical flight of fancy—perhaps two real-world examples will provide the necessary grounding. Both come from Shumaker's (2011b) report of site visits to successful embedded librarians. A librarian at a nonprofit corporation spent a great deal of time selecting and analyzing new technical articles and reports for a news alerting service. The librarian, and the information services management, became aware of a new outsourcing option that could substitute for much of this labor. Upon testing the new option, they recommended it to the manager of the information user group, and it was adopted. The embedded librarian was freed from this work—but not laid off. Instead, new, higher-value tasks were assigned. In the second example, a librarian at a law firm was assigned to manage a database relating to a new regulatory issue being tracked by the firm. For a period, the librarian devoted a substantial amount of time to this responsibility and, as a result, made an important contribution to the firm's efforts to establish its position as a leader in this new area. Eventually, however, an information vendor started to provide an acceptable alternative. Although the activity was outsourced, the librarian in this example was not laid off either but continued with other high-value contributions to the work of the firm.

One other point, sometimes missed, needs to be emphasized—the importance of relationships. An increasing body of evidence, largely based on the groundbreaking work of Tversky and Kahneman (1974), demonstrates that decision making—in management, just as in everyday life—is at best only partly rational. It follows that all the objective justifications in the world may not matter if there are no personal relationships that establish credibility with decision makers.

Summing up, the outlook for embedded librarianship in corporate and specialized organizations depends on the ability of library managers and embedded librarians to do several things. Turning a different light on Matarazzo and Pearlstein's predictive model, here are five conditions for the sustainment and growth of embedded librarianship:

- Establish relationships with key decision makers at all levels.
- Ensure that the quality and value of the embedded librarians' contribution to the organization continues to increase.
- Lead the drive to perform necessary functions by the most cost-effective means available, whether in-house or by outside providers.
- Adopt evaluation practices that are consistent with the parent organization's management culture.
- In a financial crisis, seek to be part of the solution, not part of the problem.

These themes will be developed further in Part II of this book, which addresses practices for developing and sustaining embedded librarianship.

Summary

This chapter used the available literature, fragmentary as it is, to assemble an overview of the development and key characteristics of embedded librarianship in corporations and other specialized settings such as government agencies, nonprofit organizations, and professional partnerships.

The available information indicates that embedded librarians in these organizations share an emphasis on establishing and maintaining strong working relationships. On the other hand, they perform a diverse array of information- and knowledge-related tasks.

The expansion of embedded librarianship in corporations and other specialized settings has taken place against a backdrop of downsizing and closures of traditional corporate and specialized libraries. In some organizations where the library organization has been abolished, embedded librarians continue to operate as valued employees within information user groups. However, doing so may deprive them of the opportunity to network with other information professionals. Many of the future opportunities for librarians in these types of organizations may be to operate according to the embedded model, whether as members of a central library organization or an informal network of professionals.

References

Barreau, D. 2004. The new information professional: Goldspiel grant recipient compares vision to practice. *Information Outlook* 8 (4): 31–35.

Bauwens, M. 1993. *The cybrarians manifesto.* Business Information review. Available from listserv.uh edu/cgi-bin/wa?A2=ind9304C&L–PACS-L&P=R3879& I=-3 (Accessed April 20, 2012.)

Boyd, S. 2002. A traditional library goes virtual. *Online* 26 (2): 41–45.

Dano, R., and G. McNeely. 2011. Embedded librarianship part 1: Aligning with organisational strategy to transform information into knowledge. FreePint, Ltd. [database online]. Available from web.fumsi.com/go/article/use/63659?goback =.gde_108118_member_44064318. (Accessed April 4, 2012.)

Davenport, T. H., and L. Prusak. 1993. Blow up the corporate library. *International Journal of Information Management* 13: 405–412.

Dempsey, K. 2002. Visibility: Decloaking "the invisible librarian." *Searcher* 10 (7): 76–81.

Heinze, J. S. 2010. Leveraging internal partnerships for library success. *Information Outlook* 14 (1): 13–15.

Matarazzo, J., and T. Pearlstein. 2007. Corporate score: Marrying two expert tools will help you sustain your corporate library. *Library Journal* (February 1) 132 (2): 42–43.

———. 2009. Scenario planning as preventative medicine: The case of the unexpected takeover. *Searcher* 17 (10): 26–30.

———. 2010. Survival lessons for libraries: Staying afloat in turbulent waters. *Searcher* 18 (4): 14–16, 18, 48–53.

Matthews, J. 2003. Determining and communicating the value of the special library. *Information Outlook* 7 (3): 26–31.

Montgomery, L. 2010. Thriving on turbulence: Three questions to help keep yourself grounded. *Searcher* 18 (4): 46–47.

Moore, M. 2006. Embedded in systems engineering: How one organization makes it work. *Information Outlook* 10 (5): 23–25.

Pearlstein, T., and J. M. Matarazzo. 2009a. Survival lessons for libraries: Alternate sourcing: A critical component of your survival toolkit. *Searcher* 17 (8): 32–39.

———. 2009b. Survival lessons for libraries: Corporate libraries—A soft analysis and a warning. *Searcher* 17 (6): 14–17, 52.

Peverley, J. 2005. Embedding researchers in case teams: The Bain & Company experience. PowerPoint presentation at SLA Annual Conference, Toronto, ON.

Shumaker, D., 2006. Moving to client-embedded services: Building and sustaining embedded information services. Paper presented at Special Libraries Association Conference Seminar, Baltimore, MD.

———. 2011a. Beyond instruction: Creating new roles for embedded librarians. In *Embedded librarians: Moving beyond one-shot instruction*, eds. C. Kvenild and K. Calkins, 17–30. Chicago, IL: Association of College and Research Libraries.

———. 2011b. *Models of embedded librarianship: Addendum 2011*. Alexandria, VA: Special Libraries Association.

Shumaker, D., and J. Strand. 2009. Changing your game through alignment. *Information Outlook* 13 (7): 41–44.

Shumaker, D., and M. Talley. 2009. *Models of embedded librarianship: Final report*. Alexandria, VA: Special Libraries Association.

Shumaker, D., and L. Tyler. 2007. Embedded library services: An initial inquiry into practices for their development, management, and delivery. Paper presented at Special Libraries Association Annual Conference.

Spencer, F. G. 2009. 10 questions: Reece Dano. *Information Outlook* 13 (3): 26–29.

Trimble, J. S. 2010. Reflecting corporate strategy: MITRE's information services clusters. *Information Outlook* 14 (1): 23–25.

Tversky, A., and D. Kahneman. 1974. Judgment under uncertainty: Heuristics and biases. *Science* 185 (4157): 1124–1131. Available from www.jstor.org/stable/1738360. (Accessed September 12, 2011.)

Chapter 6

Embedded Librarians in Schools and Public Libraries

This survey of embedded librarianship in different settings concludes with an examination of its application in primary and secondary education and in public libraries. Each of these two sectors has unique characteristics, as distinct from one another as they both are from the higher education, medical, and corporate sectors reviewed in the preceding chapters. In neither case does the literature use the word *embedded* to describe the innovations taking place. Yet in both, changes are happening that have elements in common with the idea of embedded librarianship.

Primary and Secondary Education

Given schools' focus on teaching and learning, it's natural that school librarians have turned to teachers as natural collaborators and partners. In the U.S., the idea that school librarians should take a role in developing and delivering the instructional program dates at least to the 1950s. However, as Craver (1986) pointed out in her review of the literature, the rhetoric has consistently outrun the reality. Despite the pronouncements of academics and professional groups, many librarians prefer administering the library to collaborating in classroom instruction or have been unable to overcome resistance to their efforts on the part of administrators and teachers. Pickard cited a 1981 study in the state of Texas that found that "school library media specialists ranked competencies associated with consultation, instruction, and utilization (instructional development) very low in importance to effective job performance and skill development as compared with the more-traditional roles of organization, management, acquisition, and dissemination" (Pickard, 1993, para. 7).

Still, progress happened over the decades, and the "school librarian" of the early- and mid-20th century became the school library media specialist of the 1980s and more recently the teacher–librarian of the 21st century. The change in terminology reflects a real shift in emphasis—from traditional print library collection development and custody to a broad range of educational media and the technologies associated with them and to an increased emphasis on the librarian's teaching role and on collaboration with classroom teachers.

Two important documents mark the milestones in this evolution. Issued by the American Association of School Librarians and the Association for Educational Communications & Technology, both have the title *Information Power*.

The first, issued in 1988, bore the subtitle *Guidelines for School Library Media Programs* (American Association of School Librarians, 1988). It incorporated recommendations that point toward embedding information literacy instruction into the curriculum. This document articulated three roles for the media specialist—information specialist, teacher, and instructional consultant. Interpreting the guidelines, Barron and Bergen (1992) declared, "the school library media specialist should be a master teacher, able to work with classroom teachers to integrate information management skills into their curriculum and classes" (p. 523). The thinking among school library media writers at the time developed the ideas that information literacy is learned best in the context of specific subjects rather than as a standalone skill—paralleling the line of thinking adopted by instructional librarians in higher education. The profession also began to articulate the concept of partnership between the media specialist and the classroom teacher.

As these ideas developed, they gave rise to the second *Information Power* document, which was subtitled *Building Partnerships for Learning* (American Association of School Librarians, 1998). The subtitle reveals the subtle but fundamental shift in thinking that had taken place in the 10-year interval between the two publications. Writing in the year after the publication of this update, Muronaga and Harada (1999) succinctly characterized the shift:

> Consultation generally designates one person, the consultant, as the "expert." ... It typically denotes an inequality of status between professionals, usually with the implication that the classroom teacher is less qualified ... to provide input and

resolve problems. ... Effective collaboration, on the other hand, depends on different-but-equal status between professionals. (para. 3)

This collaboration is exactly the relationship developed by successful embedded librarians in higher education with their subject faculty, by informationists in health sciences with clinicians, and by corporate embedded librarians with fellow professionals. It has continued to be the ideal in the school library media literature ever since.

Two factors differentiate it from embedded librarianship as seen in other settings. The first is a lack of specialization. Because of the small number of media center staff in any school, a teacher–librarian tends to work with all subjects and all grades. The second is that, consistently, the media center continues as the home base of the librarian and a learning destination for students and teachers. The teacher–librarian also continues to have an office in the media center, not colocated with the teachers of any particular subject or grade—an arrangement driven by the typical physical layout of school buildings.

Leaving those factors aside, Muronaga, a library media specialist, and Harada (1999), a library science educator, vividly characterized the nature of relationship building and collaboration between the librarian and teachers. They noted that the first task is to build trust. A good way to start is for the librarian to volunteer for activities beyond the scope of the media center. Activities like participating in the curriculum committee, helping to plan the school fair, or serving as an advisor for a student club, bring the librarian into contact with teachers and provide the opportunity to build collegial relationships.

Muronaga and Harada (1999) outlined three successive levels of partnership. Starting with receptive teachers, Muronaga established a "simple" level of collaboration by informally linking her lessons to class topics. She progressed to "deeper levels of joint planning, delivery and assessment of instruction by linking her efforts with school priorities." Ultimately, she achieved "total" collaboration, "where faculty members discuss how best to weave content area concepts and information literacy skills into integrated learning experiences for students" (para. 15).

Muronaga continued to provide leadership across a range of initiatives. For example, she facilitated the process of adding a technology coordinator to the school staff, to provide technology training and integration for the classroom teachers. Ultimately, a process evolved by which the media specialist and the technology coordinator met with classroom teachers at the beginning of each semester to coordinate curriculum and related contributions. There is a striking similarity between this strategic approach and that of academic librarians engaged in curriculum development (Muronaga and Harada, 1999).

Muronaga and Harada (1999) concluded their article with several principles of collaboration in any setting:

- Different members of the community bring different, complementary skills and knowledge (as articulated by Page and discussed in Chapter 2).
- Individuals approach planning and collaboration differently, so the librarian has to adapt to different working styles.
- The different professionals share responsibility for activities and assessment—in this case, helping students to learn.
- Planning is nonlinear; or, adjustments have to be made during the course of the project, based on experiences.

These ideas are appropriate to any organizational setting.

In succeeding years, contributions to the literature by working media specialists have demonstrated that, in some schools at least, the idea of collaboration has taken hold and media specialists are functioning much like embedded librarians in other sectors. Their collaborations have occurred in a variety of subjects and at a variety of grade levels. Here are a few examples to illustrate that diversity:

- Johnson (2005) described an ongoing partnership with a middle school social studies teacher.
- Gess (2009) related her experience collaborating with a sixth grade science teacher.
- Dees, et al. (2010) presented experiences of librarians collaborating with classroom teachers at several elementary schools in Georgia.
- Cohen (2010) described her experiences collaborating with social studies and science teachers at a secondary school in Connecticut.

Finally, paralleling another theme discussed in Chapter 3, Meyer (2010) described the involvement of a school library media specialist in a statewide initiative in social studies curriculum development. The initiative involved developing Classroom Based Assessments, a series of tasks and activities that fulfill mandated learning goals. Because the goals placed a great deal of emphasis on the ability to work with social studies information, the contribution of teacher–librarians was essential.

With the growth of interest in collaboration, there have also been efforts to evaluate the contributions of teacher–librarians to student success. Dr. Keith Curry Lance, who led statewide studies in Colorado and other states, summarized the research findings by saying that "students perform better academically where the library media specialist" meets the following conditions:

- Is part of a planning and teaching team with the classroom
- Teaches information literacy
- Provides one-to-one tutoring for students in need (Lance, 2001, para. 5)

Marcoux (2007) characterized the findings by stating that "test scores were directly impacted in relationship to the degree to which library media specialists and classroom teachers worked together" and "collaboration between teachers and library media specialists is more likely when the library media specialist is a school leader" (p. 20). Following up a study conducted by Lance and others in the state of Michigan, Mardis and Hoffman (2007) analyzed the relationship of school library media services to students' performance on standardized tests in the sciences. They found that the presence of collaboration between the library media specialist and the science classroom teacher was a significant factor associated with student success. An ongoing series of reports sponsored by Scholastic Publishing summarized the findings of studies in many states. Among the summary findings are that school library programs are effective when the following conditions are met:

- Library media specialists collaborate with classroom teachers to teach and integrate literature and information skills into the curriculum.

- Library media specialists partner with classroom teachers on projects that help students use a variety of resources, conduct research, and present their findings.
- Library media specialists are supported fiscally and programmatically by the educational community to achieve (*School Libraries Work!*, 2008, p. 6).

On a smaller scale, Beard and Antrim (2010) reported an interesting research study of students in one class who were reading below grade level. They found that when students could select their own books to read, they tended to choose books that were too difficult for them. As a result, they became frustrated and did not get the reading practice they needed. But when the classroom teacher and the librarian collaborated, and the librarian began to help students select books that were at the right level of difficulty, the students were more comfortable with the choices, they completed more books, and reading scores improved.

Although the evidence has been growing that collaboration between library media specialist and classroom teacher results in better learning results, a number of writers have noted obstacles to expanding it. The obstacles range from ingrained habits, attitudes, and preconceptions of school administrators, teachers, and librarians to librarians' lack of subject knowledge, especially in the sciences. Another issue that interferes with acceptance of the idea is the inherent vagueness of the word *collaboration*. In other words, some of the same issues arise in primary and secondary education as in higher education and other areas.

Because collaboration has become so important to the professional strategy of media specialists, the U.S. Institute of Museum and Library Services funded a large-scale effort to "understand the dynamics of collaborative partnerships between library media specialists and classroom teachers through a systematic investigation of the partnerships established" (Todd, 2008, p. 55) The study identified three levels of partnership, from least extensive to most extensive: cooperation, coordination, and true collaboration. It found that some librarians had little or no involvement at any level, and for most others, involvement was concentrated at the lower end of the scale. Todd's report of the project concluded with the following seven "insights," which are more exhortations than a systematic relationship-building process:

1. Get over helplessness and grab the opportunities to develop and implement strategic collaborations.

2. Where there is a will there is a way.

3. Giving up is not a solution.

4. The sum of the parts is greater than the whole.

5. Plan with mutuality of intent.

6. Plan with clarity of intent.

7. Focus on collaboration as reflective learning (Todd, 2008, para. 15).

The development of school librarians toward greater collaboration with classroom teachers has proceeded independently but to a great extent has paralleled the development of embedded librarianship in other sectors of the profession. Innovative school library media specialists are engaged in planning lessons, designing instructions, and delivering information literacy instruction embedded in the curriculum. They are participating in the shaping of the curriculum itself. Yet even though there is a comprehensive, federally funded program dedicated to spreading the concept, the goal of full membership in the instructional team remains elusive for many. Writing in 2008, Todd observed, "Growing research evidence … suggests collaboration is more an elusive dream rather than an established and seamless practice" (para. 7).

In the years since, prospects seem to have dimmed, not brightened. The economic Great Recession that began in 2008 contracted the budgets of state and local governments, and many positions for librarians were eliminated. Lance (2010) has documented a 12 percent decline in positions in the state of Colorado from school year 2007–2008 to 2009–2010, for example. An article in the June 24, 2011 *New York Times* (Santos, 2011) suggested that the persistence of old patterns of work, and old conceptions of the librarians' role, may be contributing factors that make it easy for politicians and administrators to dispense with librarians. The article noted that despite a state regulation mandating that a librarian be on the staff of every secondary school, half those schools no longer employ librarians. The school system's chief academic officer was quoted as saying that librarians work "in a support capacity"—in other words, not as full partners. The same officer also advanced the justification that the availability of digital information eliminates the need to visit the library— and by extension, to engage the librarian in learning. The president of the

American Association of School Libraries was quoted in the article defending the library as "the one place every kid in the school can go to learn" (para. 10), but, regrettably, the idea of the librarian embedded as a key member of the instructional team was never mentioned. It seems as if, with limited exceptions, embedded librarianship in primary and secondary schools is more a concept than a reality. The current trend makes it more important than ever to implement the new model and for school library media specialists to become full, embedded participants in the educational team.

Public Libraries

It might seem as if the idea of embedded librarianship would have no place in public libraries. If the fully developed embedded model involves close working relationships between the librarian and information users, collaboration in cognitively diverse teams, and shared responsibility for achieving common goals, how it can apply in a public library setting is problematic. This kind of arrangement might even appear inimical to the service ethic of public libraries, which emphasizes equitable service to all and affirms user privacy. If there is a distance between the public librarian and the information user, it's at least partially by design.

In every other setting analyzed thus far, there is a well-defined organization for the librarian to be embedded in. The academic librarian has the college or university and its departments and institutes. The informationist has the medical school and its various faculties. The corporate or government librarian has the corporation, the firm, or the agency, with departments, practice groups, and bureaus. The school library media specialist has the school. But the public librarian doesn't have anything like any of these. All the public librarian has is the community. The community is hardly well-defined; instead, it's an amorphous, roiling mix of population segments, community groups, and institutions of all kinds. It hardly seems possible for the public librarian to become embedded in something so diffuse.

And yet, the idea of embedded public librarians is not completely alien. If only in a metaphorical sense, it has been suggested that the public librarian can and should be an embedded librarian. Speaking to the 2008 annual conference of the Association for Library Services to Children, a unit of the American Library Association, the noted American pediatrician and author Dr. T. Berry Brazelton declared that librarians have an "opportunity to be part of the family system" and that they should assume the role of partnership with parents in fostering the learning and development of young children. He advocated that they should "go from being experts to fostering parents' expertise; from focusing on family deficits to family strengths; from objective involvement to empathic involvement; and from focusing on one dimensional learning to applying a holistic approach of early learning" (quoted in Voeller, 2008, p. 6). It's unlikely that Brazelton was recommending that the family invite the librarian home for dinner, yet the notion of the librarian as part of the "family system" and the shift to "empathic involvement" have some similarities to the characteristics of embeddedness.

Public librarians have also taken on embedded roles in response to emergencies and natural disasters. An example took place in the community of Nacogdoches, Texas, in August 2005, when the town was devastated by Hurricane Rita. In the hurricane's aftermath, the library was besieged by local residents seeking information on all sorts of community and relief services. In response, the staff established a website to serve as an information and referral clearinghouse. Initially, the librarians established partnerships with other information sources, such as a nursing professor at Stephen F. Austin University who had a database of community resources. Ultimately, they became active participants in an Interagency Coalition group, whereby they were able to maintain relationships with service providers and keep up with changes and new service groups (Barker, et al., 2008).

In the long run, the librarians recognized the value of a collaboratively operated clearinghouse for community services in any locale. They noted that if well maintained, it can be a vital emergency preparedness resource—it need not wait for the disaster to strike. They noted that a key benefit is "a mutually beneficial relationship with agencies (i.e., open doors for library outreach programs at agencies, and staff at agencies offer to present programs in their areas of expertise at the library)" (Barker, et al., 2008, p. 56). It is not too much to interpret this kind of involvement as a demonstration of librarian embeddedness in the network of community service providers.

Librarians can become embedded in other aspects of community life as well. One example that has gained attention in recent years is outreach to underserved groups, such as homeless persons. At the San Francisco Public Library, a library staff member paid by the city's Department of

Health coordinates the Health and Safety Associates, a group of part-time interns. Team members roam the library, offering assistance and referrals to anyone in need. Funding by the Health Department and regular interactions with a variety of social service agencies make this program a partnership in which the library plays a key role (Lilienthal, 2011).

Sometimes the embedded role of public librarians takes them outside the library's walls. In a sidebar, Lilienthal (2011) related the story of Anne Gancarz, community services librarian in Chicopee, Massachusetts, who "worked with a local nun running a shelter for recovering alcoholics and drug users who were 'essentially homeless.' Gancarz spent time in the shelter getting to know residents, many of whom felt alienated from the library" (p. 31).

These partnerships and embedded relationships ultimately lead to a holistic approach to working with the public. Librarians collaborating with other agencies begin viewing people not as "information seekers" or "information users" alone, but as individuals with information needs best addressed in a comprehensive fashion. The adoption of this mindset results in a replacement of traditional approaches to library outreach and the adoption of a community development approach. The Government of Canada's Working Together Project provides an example. In this 4-year demonstration project, "The objective was to use a community development approach to build relationships and partnerships with community individuals and groups so that the library could better understand what they wanted and needed from the institution. The hoped-for result was a model for library services that emphasized community consultation, collaboration and a willingness to change in order to meet community needs" (Working Together Project, n.d.a, para. 5).

The project resulted in a toolkit for public library personnel to engage with community members in a new way, "not simply working with people to reach their goals, but working with them to understand how the library can help them reach their goals" (Working Together Project, n.d.b, para. 11). It embodies a distinct difference from the approach taken in traditional library outreach initiatives. It shifts the focus from a one-way service delivery approach, transactional in nature, to a collaborative approach that develops the library role in consultation with individuals and groups in the community. It establishes an embedded model of librarianship in the community.

While the foregoing examples, including the Working Together Project, focus on establishing relationships with underserved members of the community, one writer has articulated a vision of embedded public librarianship that explicitly encompasses all segments of multiple communities. In perhaps the only use of the term *embedded librarianship* in the literature of public libraries, Guthrie (2011) wrote that "branch libraries reflect the concept of 'embedded librarians' which means that the librarian is located among patrons rather than in only a central location. A branch library is embedded in the neighborhood where everyday living concerns can be identified and addressed" (para. 3). Guthrie advocated that these embedded branches should function as nodes in a social network connecting the diverse neighborhoods and enhancing communication and understanding across the city. In effect, this proposal took Bauwens' idea of corporate librarians as nodes in overlapping networks, discussed in Chapter 5, and expanded it to a local community and even a global scale. As Steve Early, a community coordinator with the *Baltimore Sun* newspaper, put it, the "proposal does exactly this, and in a networked fashion, maximizing the potential generativity. Librarians and patrons ... will teach, learn from and feed off of other libraries. Library networks will teach, learn from and feed off of the web at large—and vice versa" (quoted in Guthrie, 2011, para. 6).

No known public library has even begun to build such a network of embedded branches. I hope that this idea will be explored in the future. It's just possible that, despite the apparent incompatibility of the embedded librarianship model with public libraries, the public library sector will someday become the most sophisticated example of embeddedness of all.

Summary

In this chapter, we've seen that the essence of embedded librarianship applies to librarians in primary and secondary education, and to the public library sector.

In school librarianship, the orientation to foster collaboration between librarians and classroom teachers has been advocated for a number of years, although well-developed programs of this type remain the exception rather than the rule. In the current economic and budgetary environment, the number of school librarians is being reduced in many localities. These reductions deprive school librarians of the ability to specialize to the extent that they might, but enterprising librarians are still finding opportunities to partner with classroom teachers in embedding information literacy into the curriculum. The current constraints on school librarians are especially sad in light of the evidence that has been developed pointing to their important impact on student achievement when they are able to participate as full partners with the classroom teachers. Embedded roles may be the best way forward for this segment of the library profession.

In public libraries, the notion of embedded librarianship is further from the mainstream of current practice. Still, there are examples of public library staff initiating collaborations with other community groups and agencies to further the common good in their localities. An increasing body of literature advocates this practice, and a few examples are beginning to show how it can be done.

References

American Association of School Librarians, and Association for Educational Communications and Technology. 1988. *Information power: Guidelines for school library media programs*. Chicago: American Library Association.

———. 1998. *Information power: Building partnerships for learning*. Chicago: American Library Association.

Barker, A., M. Franks, J. Hensarling, P. Reynolds, C. Shaw, and T. Sparks. 2008. Committed to the community: A community services website. *Texas Library Journal* 84 (2): 56–59.

Barron, D., and T. J. Bergen Jr. 1992. Information power: The restructured school library for the nineties. *The Phi Delta Kappan* 73 (7): 521–525.

Beard, T. M., and P. Antrim. 2010. Reading workshops are most effective with a teacher–librarian. *Teacher Librarian* 37 (5): 24–36.

Cohen, S. 2010. Growing a knowledge building center. *Teacher Librarian* 37 (5): 37–41.

Craver, K. W. 1986. The changing instructional role of the high school media specialist, 1950–84: A survey of professional literature, standards, and research studies. *School Library Media Quarterly* 14 (4).

Dees, D., A. Mayer, H. Morin, and E. Willis. 2010. Librarians as leaders in professional learning communities through technology, literacy and collaboration. *Library Media Connection* (October): 10.

Gess, A. 2009. Collaboration: Finding the teacher, finding the topic, finding the time. *Library Media Connection* 27 (4): 24.

Guthrie, L. 2011. Branch libraries as social network for Tulsa. *Oklahoma Eagle*, January 31.

Johnson, M. J. 2005. Collaborating to improve social studies instruction: A case study. *Library Media Connection* 23 (4): 22.

Lance, K. C. 2001. Proof of the power: Quality library media programs affect academic achievement. *MultiMedia & Internet @ Schools.* www.infotoday.com/ mmschools/sep01/lance.htm. (Accessed December 17, 2011.)

———. 2010. *Endorsed librarian positions in Colorado Public Schools trending downward.* Denver, CO: Colorado Department of Education, ED3/110.10/No. 288.

Lilienthal, S. M. 2011. The problem is not the homeless. *Library Journal* (June 15): 30–34.

Marcoux, B. 2007. Levels of collaboration: Where does your work fit in. *School Library Media Activities Monthly* 24 (4): 20.

Mardis, M., and E. Hoffman. 2007. Collection and collaboration: Science in Michigan middle school media centers. *School Library Media Research* 10. Retrieved from www.eric.ed.gov/ERICWebPortal/detail?accno=EJ851700 (Accessed December 17, 2011.)

Meyer, N. 2010. Collaboration success for student achievement in social studies: The Washington State story. *Teacher Librarian* 37 (4): 40.

Muronaga, K., and V. Harada. 1999. Building teaching partnerships: The art of collaboration. *Teacher Librarian* 27 (1): 9–14.

Pickard, P. W. 1993. Current research: The instructional consultant role of the school library media specialist. *School Library Media Quarterly* 21 (2). www.ala.org/ aasl/aaslpubsandjournals/slmrb/editorschoiceb/infopower/selctpickard. (Accessed April 23, 2012.)

Santos, F. 2011. In lean times, schools squeeze out librarians. *New York Times,* June 24, 2011. www.nytimes.com/2011/06/25/nyregion/schools-eliminating-librarians-as-budgets-shrink.html?_r=2&rcf=education. (Accessed July 6, 2011.)

School libraries work!. 2008. Scholastic Publishing. Available from www.scholastic. com/content/collateral_resources/pdf/s/slw3_2008.pdf. (Accessed April 4, 2012.)

Todd, R. 2008. Collaboration: From myth to reality. Let's get down to business. Just do it! *School Library Monthly* 24 (7): 54–58.

Voeller, S. L. 2008. Brazelton encourages librarians to be part of the family. *ALA Cognotes* (4) (July 1): 6.

Working Together Project. n.d.a. Background: Thinking about the public library. Human Resources and Social Development Canada [database online]. Available from www.librariesincommunities.ca/?page_id=10. (Accessed April 4, 2012.)

———. n.d.b. Community development in a library context. Human Resources and Social Development Canada [database online]. Available from www.librariesin communities.ca/?page_id=3. (Accessed April 4, 2012.)

PART 2

Your Path to Success

In Part 2, the focus shifts from the broad field of librarianship to you, your organization, and your job. No matter what is going on in other organizations, yours has unique characteristics, and your embedded librarianship program must fit the climate and culture where you work. The good news is that there are tools and approaches that you can apply as you develop a strategy to create, strengthen, and sustain your embedded role. In Part 2, we'll explore these common tools and approaches.

The first step is assessment. It's important to start by understanding how far along you and your organization are on the path to embedded librarianship. Next, you'll want to identify the conditions in your environment that are either favorable or unfavorable to developing your role further. In Chapter 7, we will explore these questions and show how you can apply an analytical framework to assessing your current position and the readiness of your library and your organization to take further steps.

Chapter 8 is all about getting started. It is written especially for those just setting out on the journey to embedded librarianship, planning an initiative to reach new information users, or leading librarians who have not worked in embedded roles in the past. If your self-assessment tells you that it's time to start something new, then Chapter 8 offers an approach to developing an action plan and putting it into practice.

Like any successful initiative, successful embedded librarianship has to be consciously and systematically sustained over time. It isn't something that can be started up and then left to run itself. In Chapter 9, we draw on the research to present the practices of successful embedded librarians and leaders and offer tools for you to adapt those practices to your environment.

One of the characteristics shared by most successful embedded librarians is that they have measures and evaluations in place by which they can gauge their success. The journey to embedded librarianship would be incomplete without a discussion of evaluating your success. In Chapter 10, we bring the development process full circle by offering guidelines and practices from the leaders, so that you can adapt them to the measurement of your own success.

Chapter 7

Assessing Your Readiness

"What makes you an embedded librarian?"

There is no single, simple answer to this question. Embedded librarianship has multiple attributes—it isn't a simple either/or proposition. Instead, it's a range of behaviors that lead to degrees or levels of embeddedness. Being an embedded librarian involves having a strong working relationship with an information user group. It means contributing to the work of that user group by applying your information management knowledge and skills. It's about being an "integral part to the whole," as Jezmynne Dene put it. But to find out what specific activities characterize an embedded librarian, it's necessary to get behind those generalities.

Indicators of Embeddedness

The research suggests four broad themes that mark embedded librarians. They interact frequently with their information user groups, and these interactions involve communicating both about work-related topics and for social purposes. They collaborate with members of their groups, whether through research and information analysis, content management and stewardship, instruction and co-teaching, or the application of other information skills. They receive feedback from the information users about the value of their work. And they connect with the leaders of their information user groups to get direction, feedback, and support (Shumaker and Talley, 2009).

The survey that follows asks questions about these behaviors. You can use this questionnaire for yourself—if you are a solo librarian or an individual contributor—or for a group if you supervise a staff of librarians. To gain an estimate of where you, or the library staff in your organization, are on the journey of embedded librarianship, take the survey. Then after you score your results, read further to explore their meaning.

Embedded Librarianship
Maturity Questionnaire

The following table lists some attributes and practices commonly associated with embedded librarians. Circle the number in the appropriate column to indicate the frequency with which each is found in your organization. Copy the number you circled to the right-hand column, and add the numbers to calculate your score.

For each attribute, answer for yourself alone or for librarians in general in your organization, whichever is more appropriate.

During the past year, have you:

Attribute	Frequently or a Routine Practice	Occasionally or Not a Routine Practice	Rarely or Never	Score
1. Collaborated with one or more members of a group outside the library; contributed to their work directly on an ongoing basis?	15	8	0	
2. Met more than once with members of an information user group to discuss information needs and present results to them?	12	6	0	
3. Provided information literacy instruction (knowledge of information resources or information handling and management techniques) away from library facilities, such as in an office, a conference room, or classroom?	12	6	0	
4. Met (in person or virtually) with senior members (e.g., executives, managers, supervisors) of your information user group to discuss information-related needs and services of the group?	10	5	0	
5. Attended a meeting, class, or conference devoted to the area of your information user group's expertise (not oriented to librarians)?	10	5	0	
6. Attended meetings of an information user group to learn about its work and information needs?	10	5	0	
7. Collaborated on or contributed to the electronic communications and/or collaborative workspaces of an information user group, including email, wikis, blogs, course management sites, and other web-based workspaces?	10	5	0	
8. Had lunch with members of your customer group?	8	4	0	
9. Attended social events held by your customer group?	8	4	0	
10. Met with the manager of an information user group to discuss your performance and your contributions to the group?	5	3	0	

Interpreting Your Score

The questions in this survey are based on those asked of embedded librarians in the *Models of Embedded Librarianship* research project (Shumaker and Talley, 2009; see Appendix A). They also align closely with the four themes of embedded librarians' success:

- Communicating and promoting
- Delivering highly sophisticated, customized, value-added services
- Evaluating the impact of embedded librarians and communicating with decision makers
- Engaging with management

The weighting of the 10 questions is based on the frequency of positive responses in the research project's initial survey of embedded librarians. In other words, the more points assigned to a question, the more likely it was that an embedded librarian in the survey would answer yes. These questions are intended as a general guideline, not as a specific statistical measure.

For convenience, you can segment the continuum of embedded librarianship into four zones of maturity:

- If you scored between 81 and 100 points, you are *highly embedded*. At this stage, librarians have formed close working relationships with one or more information user groups. They communicate regularly with the leader and members of the groups, work closely with them on projects, and are recognized as integral members of the group. They contribute complex, highly professional work to the group and are trusted for their commitment and expertise.
- If your score was between 51 and 80 points, you are probably in the process of *developing* embedded relationships. Collaboration has been established between librarians and one or more information user groups. One or more librarians are developing an understanding of the work of the group or groups, and there are opportunities for communication. The contributions of the librarian are growing in complexity and

value, and the librarian is gaining recognition and trust from the information user-group management and members.

- Scores in the range of 21 to 50 points probably indicate *emerging* embedded relationships. At this level, a few beginning steps have been taken toward the embedded model. A librarian may have been engaged in the work of an information user group on a trial basis. An information user-group manager may have expressed interest in having a librarian work more closely with the group, or library management may have begun to reach out to key contacts.

- Finally, if your score is in the 0-to-20-point range, you're *not embedded*. At this stage, library services are delivered according to a traditional service model. Services are transactional in nature. Librarians do not have ongoing relationships with specific information user groups, and the leaders of groups do not actively engage the librarians in their work. Opportunities for librarians to collaborate and to contribute highly complex, value-added work to the groups are very limited. Librarians' knowledge of the mission and goals of key groups in the organization is also limited.

Table 7.1 summarizes these maturity levels of embedded librarianship.

Table 7.1   Maturity Levels of Embedded Librarianship

Point Range	Embedded Librarianship Maturity Level
81–100	*Highly Embedded*: Librarians have formed strong working relationships with staff and management of one or more information user groups and collaborate closely with them.
51–80	*Developing*: Some collaborative relationships have been established and may be growing.
21–50	*Emerging*: There are limited collaborative relationships and perhaps some interest in strengthening collaboration and engagement.
0–20	*Not Embedded*: Your library is operating pretty much on the traditional library service model.

Assessing Your Readiness for Change

Now that you have assessed your current level of embeddedness, you're ready to evaluate your readiness to increase it. The two characteristics, current embeddedness and readiness to grow, are not the same. Embarking on a strategy to introduce or expand embedded librarianship is a change management process similar to any other. Change management is a dangerous undertaking, and it's wise to assess conditions carefully before you begin. As Machiavelli said, "There is nothing more difficult to take in hand, more perilous to conduct, or more uncertain in its success, than to take the lead in the introduction of a new order of things" (Machiavelli, 1952).

As you review your answers to the Embedded Librarianship Maturity Questionnaire, you may notice one or more areas that need work, and perhaps one or more that are already strengths for you. Perhaps you have the ability to produce complex, customized, and highly valued work but not the visibility and relationships you need in order to demonstrate your value. Or perhaps you have luncheon companions who work in important information user groups, but their managers don't recognize the value a librarian could add to the organization. Or perhaps you are new to the organization and don't really understand the work of key groups. These are examples of readiness factors. Your situation may be strong in some areas but weak in others. There may be some factors that are in your favor but others that must be addressed. As you begin to plan, you'll do well to take an inventory of these strengths and weaknesses.

Even if you are already at the highly embedded level and you've already succeeded in establishing one or more strong embedded relationships, you may be seeking more opportunities to expand your embedded role. In all my research, I have yet to find an embedded librarian who feels that all the opportunities in the organization have been fully explored. So even if you, or your library staff, have strong embedded relationships already, you may want to assess your readiness to expand into new areas.

Broadly, there are two major factors that contribute to readiness for starting or expanding an embedded librarianship program: readiness of the librarian and readiness of the organization. Elements of librarians' readiness include the following:

- Skill sets and level of professional mastery
- Understanding of the subject domain of target information user groups
- Understanding of the political and organizational context of the target groups
- Interest, ability, and motivation to do outreach and to form strong, collaborative working relationships

Organizational readiness includes these elements:

- Interest and support of an executive champion, who sees the value, or potential value, of embedded librarianship
- Good middle-management relationships between the library manager and information user-group managers
- Enthusiastic library users who are also highly respected among their peers and management
- A management culture that supports delegation and autonomy at the middle and lower levels and that encourages experimentation and innovation

Now let's examine each of these factors in turn.

Elements of Librarian Readiness

First, embedded librarians have to be good librarians. Embedded librarianship is no place for the novice or the librarian whose skills aren't well-developed. An embedded librarian is highly visible and can't hide mediocre work. The embedded librarian has to be effective. Successful embedded librarians have to be capable of making sophisticated, complex, highly valuable contributions to their organizations. The exact nature of those contributions, and of the skill set that is demanded, vary with the needs of the information user organization. In an academic setting, as seen in Chapter 3, instructional development and delivery skills are likely to be required. The librarian who has no idea how to develop an information literacy instructional program is probably going to struggle in this setting. If classroom instruction is required, the librarian who is uncomfortable with public speaking and teaching is not ready for the opportunity. In other settings, sophisticated research and analysis, content management skills, or taxonomy development may be required. The future embedded librarian must be confident and ready for these responsibilities. To mitigate this demand, some information and library managers are able to provide mentoring. Less-experienced librarians may be hired to work in a central information center and given opportunities to embed in projects and work with more-experienced embedded librarians as their skills develop.

Successful embedded librarians need an understanding of both the subject domain and the organizational context of the information user group. It's important to understand and speak the language of the information user group. If the subject is financial management, for example, the librarian who doesn't know the difference between revenue and profit will not be trusted to make important judgments. In the *Models of Embedded Librarianship* research project, we found that only about half of embedded librarians have prior education or experience before beginning their embedded assignments (Shumaker and Talley, 2009). However, those who don't have the necessary understanding before taking the job have to acquire it rapidly. Whether through self-education and independent reading, mentoring, attending conferences, or formal education, they "get up to speed" and stay there. As seen in Chapter 6, some organizations require embedded librarians to engage in continuing education to keep their domain knowledge sharp.

Knowledge of organizational politics and context is just as important as, but distinct from, knowledge of a business or technical domain. The trusted embedded librarian has to "know the ropes"—understand "how things work." in order to make the independent judgments that are expected. For this reason, some organizations put librarians through the same orientation that is given to faculty, attorneys, or other professionals. These orientations often provide the opportunity to meet and hear from the top executives of the organization and to make acquaintances among other new employees, as well as gain insights into the history, culture, strategy, and operations of the organization.

The last element of librarian readiness is the ability and motivation to reach out and form relationships that lead to embedded librarianship. This can be the most challenging element for experienced staff who are used to traditional library service operations. Often, veteran staff members are veterans because they like things as they are and work well within the boundaries of traditional service modes. Their skills may be excellent. Their knowledge of the organization, particularly the informal networks and office grapevine, may be sophisticated. They may relish the casual relationships they have formed with employees who habitually drop in at the library. But if they are not eager to make a fundamental change, take risks, and reach out, then their efforts to become embedded librarians are likely to fall short. They may "backslide" into their traditional modes of service, or they may simply quit. Both have happened in situations where an entire staff of reference librarians has been told to become embedded librarians.

Elements of Organizational Readiness

Why assess the readiness of the organization? It's obvious that librarians' readiness is important, because no embedded librarianship initiative can succeed if the librarians lack the capability or the motivation to carry it out. But why assess the rest of the organization? What is it responsible for?

The answer goes back to the characteristics of embedded librarianship discussed in Chapter 1. Embedded librarianship is a partnership. It isn't something that the librarians do *to* the rest of the organization; it's something they do *with* other members of the organization. To have a partnership, you have to have a partner. So when you assess the readiness of the organization, you are really assessing whether conditions are favorable for the librarians to form new partnerships with groups of information users.

The first two elements of organizational readiness have to do with management relationships. In some cases, executive champions who see the value of librarians can encourage the development of embedded relationships for librarians. An example of this is Jill Stover Heinze, profiled in Chapter 1. Heinze's relationship with the Brand Communications Group began when the president of the company initiated her move into the group's office area. Another example from my experience occurred when I presented a briefing on library services to the executive group of an operating center of the company where I worked. At the conclusion of the briefing, the senior vice president and general manager of the unit asked what I needed from him in order to foster stronger relationships between the unit and the librarians. The resulting dialog led to further communication and opened the door to more conversations and initiatives with different parts of the unit.

On the other hand, midlevel relationships are essential, too. A respected manager who values the contributions of an embedded librarian and encourages staff to involve librarians in tasks is a much more effective promoter for the librarian than all the flyers any librarian could produce. A manager who is open to and available for a peer-to-peer discussion of ways to strengthen library services may be the partner for a pilot project that can demonstrate the value of embedded librarianship to others in the organization.

The third element is the presence of respected professionals who are avid library users. These users, who are not necessarily managers, can be valuable guides to opportunities for expanding embedded librarianship. After all, not everyone in an organization needs an embedded librarian. The nature of work varies. Not every course in a university has a strong research component or serves as a focal point for developing students' information literacy skills. But a respected instructor who has already asked for input on designing a research assignment, and whose students are already finding their way to the library, is likely to be the instructor who would be interested in a formal embedded relationship. A respected scientist or a successful marketer who already relies heavily on library services may be an indicator that others in the same research group or marketing team would also benefit from a formalized embedded relationship. These professionals may not be able to mandate or lead an initiative, but they may be willing to influence their managers and colleagues to consider it.

Whereas the first three elements are all about willingness to act, the fourth deals with the ability to act. Individuals at different strata of the organization may be interested in initiating embedded librarianship, but their willingness is likely to be wasted if they don't have the ability to take a risk and to do something new and different. Some organizations are mired in the status quo. Initiatives of the executive are watered down or subverted by personnel in the middle and lower ranks. Other organizations are hamstrung by a command and control orientation or even micromanagement. Midlevel managers and staff are unable to get approval for changes they want to make. Innovation gets weighed down with reviews and approvals until it grinds to a halt. Especially if embedded librarianship represents something brand new for the organization, these conditions are unfavorable, to say the least. What's needed, instead, is an organizational climate that encourages moderate, well-considered risk taking; pilot projects; and innovative approaches that are evaluated after a reasonable time. In these organizations, whether the innovation comes from senior management or from lower levels, it gets a chance.

Following is a self-assessment questionnaire that you can use to assess both dimensions of readiness: the readiness of library staff and the readiness of the parent organization. Here's how to use it.

As you did with the Embedded Librarianship Maturity Questionnaire on page 124, enter your score on each line in the right-hand column and add up the totals. Note that you may have a mix of positive and negative numbers in the right-hand column, so be sure to subtract the negatives. You may even wind up with a negative overall score—that's OK. When you have done this for both parts of the questionnaire, you're ready for the next step, which will be shown later in Figure 7.1. For examples that illustrate how to complete the readiness assessment, see the section immediately following the Readiness Assessment Questionnaire and Worksheet.

Readiness Assessment Questionnaire and Worksheet

Use this worksheet to assess the readiness of the library staff and the parent organization to implement an embedded library services program.

In the two tables that follow, circle the number in the appropriate cell to indicate the readiness of the library staff and the parent organization. Transfer the number you circled to the right-hand column, and add the numbers to calculate your score. Be sure to subtract negative scores when calculating your overall scores. [*Author's Note:* This worksheet is loosely based on the results of research reported in Shumaker, D., & Talley, M. (2009). *Models of embedded librarianship: Final report.* Alexandria, VA: Special Libraries Association. Neither numeric values nor proportions should be considered as exact measures.]

Part 1: Library Readiness

Factor	High	Moderate	Limited or Nil	Score
Staff librarianship skills: research	20	10	−20	
Staff librarianship skills: information literacy instruction	15	5	−15	
Staff librarianship skills: content management	5	2	−5	

	High	Medium	Limited or Nil	Score
Staff knowledge and understanding of the parent organization: culture, mission, values, goals, and objectives	20	10	−20	
Staff current knowledge of subject domains of key information user groups	10	5	0	
Staff interest in and capability to learn the subject domains of key information user groups	10	0	−15	
Staff ability and interest in outreach, presentations, and relationships with information user groups	20	5	−25	
Library Readiness Total Score				

Part 2: Organizational Readiness

Factor	High	Medium	Limited or Nil	Score
Executive "champion" to support embedded services initiative	20	5	−20	
Strong current relationships with middle managers	20	5	−20	
Heavy users of library services who are respected by their peers	20	5	−20	
Autonomy of library manager and customer group managers to establish embedded relationships	20	5	−20	
Pragmatic, open, innovative management culture	20	5	−20	
Organizational Readiness Total Score				

Readiness Assessment Scenarios

This section presents four scenarios. Each one gives information that can be used to evaluate the readiness factors presented in the preceding section. Read a scenario, then assess the readiness of the library by completing the Readiness Assessment questionnaire. A suggested analysis follows each scenario.

Scenario 1

The Memorial Medical School and Hospital Library is experiencing a decline in reference requests. Staff members are concerned and eager to show the value of their work to the institution. Having read about embedded informationists in other teaching hospitals, they are eager to embed themselves in the clinical teams at Memorial. They are experienced and effective research librarians but have had few opportunities to do information literacy instruction or content management. Unfortunately, they have been somewhat isolated from other activities at the Medical School. Furthermore, the library director fears that neither her manager, the director of administration, nor the senior leaders of the hospital will be in favor of this idea. They have not been very supportive of the library. Furthermore, the chairs of many of the academic departments appear to have a strong orientation toward defending their "turf" from any encroachments. Thus the director anticipates that few if any of them will be receptive either, although if an ally could be found at the middle-management level, the director believes that an embedded relationship could be formed. The library has some very supportive regular users among the medical staff, especially in the Oncology and Pediatrics departments, but it's not clear how influential these individual doctors can be.

Analysis: Librarian readiness is high. Staff members have strong research skills (+20), but it's not clear that they have strong instructional or content management skills—they score a "moderate" on each of those dimensions (5 + 2 = 7 total). They are isolated from the mainstream of the Medical School, so they receive a –20 on that factor. However, they have good knowledge of the medical field and are highly motivated to learn more about the Medical School and engage in outreach and form relationships (+10, +10, and +20). Their overall readiness score, then, is 20 + 7 – 20 + 10 + 10 + 20 = 47.

Organizational readiness is a different story. The library has no support from senior or midlevel managers, which gives them a –20 on each of those questions. The organizational culture and autonomy are a bit uncertain, though apparently positive. They earn 5 points on each of those factors. As to the individual users who are enthusiastic and well respected—there appear to be some, but their influence is uncertain. The award is 5 points on that factor. So, the overall organizational readiness score is –20 – 20 + 5 + 5 + 5 = –25.

Scenario 2

The library of the law firm Dewey, Cheatham, and Howe is woefully understaffed, with just two library staff members to respond to the information needs of more than 200 lawyers. The senior librarian has more than 10 years' professional experience and strong in-depth research skills but joined the firm only 3 months ago. The senior librarian formerly worked as a reference supervisor in a law school and has not worked in a law firm before. The junior librarian was hired last month, immediately after receiving her library science degree. She studied both instructional development and web content management in her library science program but has not applied her skills in the workplace. She was hired for these skills and because she had done well in a legal research course. Her personality in the workplace appears to be rather quiet and reserved. The senior librarian has come to think the library is undervalued and underutilized. Few of the senior partners seem to care much about it. The senior librarian has noticed that a few in-depth, challenging research assignments have come in from a handful of partners who are highly regarded, and the librarian has received nice thank-you notes for work performed from two or three of them. Other than these few partners, the heaviest users are some of the newest associates, who seem to be casting about for any help they can get. The senior librarian would like to establish embedded relationships with major practice groups as a strategy to change these circumstances, but the librarian's boss, the library partner, has said such an initiative would have to be approved by the executive committee of the firm. Nonetheless, the librarian noticed recently that the manager of information technology and the manager of human resources jointly announced a knowledge management initiative, so the librarian wonders whether there are ways to start initiatives in the firm after all.

Analysis: Librarian readiness in this scenario is weak. Because of the senior librarian's research experience, the first factor rates the librarians a 20. Because the junior librarian is so inexperienced, the staff's instructional and content management skills both are moderate and worth 5 and 2 points, respectively. Since both librarians are quite new to the organization and lack prior law firm experience, their knowledge of organizational context is limited, which results in a –20 point value on that factor. Apart from the senior librarian's general knowledge of law librarianship, their knowledge of the specific subject domains, such as important legal practice areas, is also limited, so they earn 0 points. Similarly, the interest and capability of both librarians to learn the subject domains is unclear. At best, it can be assessed as moderate, which results in no points being awarded. Finally, because there are indications that the junior librarian in particular may not be predisposed toward outreach and forming relationships, this factor is limited or nil and assigned a value of –25 points. Taken together, the librarian readiness score is thus $20 + 5 + 2 - 20 + 0 + 0 - 25 = -18$.

As to organizational readiness, most of the indicators are negative. Both the executive-level and middle-level management appear uninterested in the library, yielding a value of –20 on each of these factors. Fortunately, there are a few heavy library users who are important partners in the firm, so this element qualifies as moderate, with a score of 5. On the other hand, the reaction of the library partner indicates that the senior librarian's autonomy is limited, so an assessment of limited or nil and a score of –20 for autonomy is warranted. Finally, although the prospects for innovation do not seem very bright, the recent initiative by the information technology and human resources managers offers a glimmer of hope, perhaps justifying a moderate rating and 5 points. Taken together, then, the organizational readiness score of Dewey, Cheatham, and Howe is $-20 - 20 + 5 - 20 + 5 = -50$.

Scenario 3

At Central Overshoe State University, a group of faculty members who teach the first-year composition course have approached the library director. They found that students do not perform well on research paper assignments. Familiar with the concepts of information literacy, they are proposing that a librarian be assigned to attend their classes, present lectures on research skills and resources, and counsel students. They have met with the library director, accompanied by their department head, to make this proposal. During the meeting, they indicated that the provost and the university president probably wouldn't care one way or the other but that senior-level support wasn't important and that the arrangement could be made among the midlevel managers in attendance. Much as the library director would like to agree to their request, the library has recently experienced a wave of retirements of senior reference staff. Remaining staff members are very inexperienced, and there are several current vacancies. Fortunately, the library director has been able to attract new reference librarians who, despite their inexperience, are energetic, outgoing, and interested in developing innovative library services.

Analysis: Central Overshoe State's situation offers contrasts with each of the preceding scenarios. Its overall librarian readiness for embedded librarianship is weak, but for different reasons than we found at Dewey,

Cheatham, and Howe. Given that the remaining reference librarians are inexperienced, they probably have limited or nil capabilities on each of the first three elements—research, information literacy instruction, and content management—for scores of –20, –15, and –5, respectively. Further, since the staff members are recent hires to the University, their knowledge of the University is also limited, for a score of –20. There is no indication that they have expertise in any critical subject domains, either, so they receive a limited rating and 0 points on that element. Things begin to look up in the last two elements on the questionnaire. Because the new staff members have been hired for their interest in innovation and outreach and for their personal qualities, which should equip them to form relationships, they deserve a high rating and scores of +10 and +20, respectively, on these elements. In all, these assessments add up to a librarian readiness score of $-20 - 15 - 5 - 20 + 0 + 10 + 20 = -30$.

Organizational readiness at Central Overshoe State also contrasts sharply with that of Memorial Medical and Dewey, Cheatham, and Howe. The University executives are uninvolved, but at least they are not hostile to the idea of embedded librarianship. That counts as moderate support and an award of 5 points. Further, the presence of the department head together with the instructors signals both strong midlevel support and the engagement of current, respected library users. These elements rank as high, with point scores of 20 for both factors. Just as positive are the indicators of autonomy and the management culture at the University. Taking the statements made in the meeting at face value, we can attribute high ratings on both these factors, again awarding 20 points for each. In all, then, the scoring of the organizational readiness of Central Overshoe is $5 + 20 + 20 + 20 + 20 = 85$, a very sharp contrast to scenarios 1 and 2.

Scenario 4

A librarian at the Department of Justice has worked closely with lawyers of the Criminal Division for several years. During this time the librarian has gained a sophisticated understanding of the work of the Division and formed close working relationships with the chief and the attorneys in a particular section. Despite the fact that the librarian must share general reference desk and virtual reference duty, the librarian has developed custom research tutorials on criminal law and is stewarding a knowledge base for Criminal Division lawyers. Now the librarian and the section chief within the Division have proposed to the library manager that the librarian's office be moved to the section's office area. The Division director has come on board and voiced support for trying the arrangement as a pilot project that could be expanded to other sections if successful. The director has offered support in the form of funding and advocacy. The librarian also recognizes that there are other experienced librarians who are developing the knowledge and relationships that would enable them to succeed.

Analysis: The Justice Department scenario contrasts sharply with the three preceding situations. Here, all systems are go, and the green light is on. The librarian's research, instruction, and content management skills are all high, and other librarians are not far behind. That garners them scores of 20, 15, and 5. Similarly, knowledge of the subject domain and the organizational context are high, earning scores of 20 and 10. Finally, the librarian's involvement in the proposal, as well as indications that other librarians may also be suited for embedded roles, suggests ratings of high and scores of 10 and 20, respectively, on the final two elements. Librarian readiness, then, comes out as 20 + 15 + 5 + 20 + 10 + 10 + 20 = 100, a perfect score.

Organizational readiness is similarly positive. The Division director is a suitable candidate for the role of executive champion, so we rate the factor high and award 20 points. The involvement of the section chief and the background information that strong working relationships have already been formed indicate high ratings and scores of 20 for both of these factors. Finally, it appears that the autonomy exists in a pragmatic culture to accomplish the needed change. We assign high ratings and 20 points to each of these elements. In all, the sum of organizational readiness scores is 20 + 20 + 20 + 20 + 20 = 100, again a perfect score. It appears that the Criminal Division is a perfect setting to develop the opportunities of embedded librarianship!

Visualizing Readiness Assessments

What is the point of all these calculations? They are not scientific measurements, after all. This section shows how the calculations can be used to visualize different combinations of librarian and organizational readiness on a simple two-dimensional graph. Chapter 8 shows how to use the resulting analysis to explore strategies that are appropriate to different situations and contexts, strategies that can be customized and applied to different organizational settings in order to develop and strengthen embedded librarianship.

To complete the analysis and the visualization, the readiness scores need to be plotted on the graph shown in Figure 7.1. Note that the *x*-, or horizontal, axis will be used for Organizational Readiness, and the *y*-, or vertical, axis for Librarian Readiness. The point at which the two axes cross is (0,0): The value of each axis at that point is zero. Each axis has a maximum value of 100 points and a minimum value of –100 points, as shown in Figure 7.1. These represent the maximum and minimum scores that could be awarded in our readiness calculations.

The key to the graph is that the quadrants define four broad conditions of readiness for embedded librarianship. Starting in the upper right, and moving counterclockwise, the quadrants and conditions of readiness align as follows:

- Quadrant 1: High organizational readiness and high librarian readiness. In this quadrant, both librarians and the organization have received positive readiness scores. Many, if not all, conditions are favorable for the development or expansion of embedded librarianship.

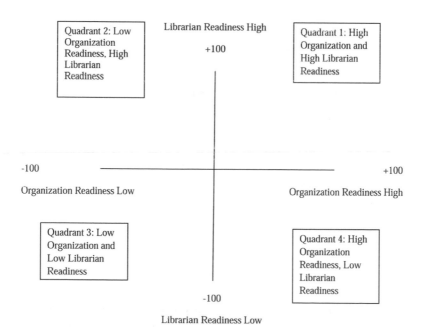

Figure 7.1   *Embedded Librarianship Readiness Graph*

- Quadrant 2: Low organizational readiness, but high librarian readiness. Here, librarians are willing and able to perform in embedded roles, but factors in the organization create obstacles to initiating or expanding embedded relationships.

- Quadrant 3: Low organizational readiness and low librarian readiness. There are few if any conditions propitious for embarking on a program to implement the embedded librarianship model. Instead, there are obstacles of capability and/or interest among the librarians, and a lack of support among one or more segments of the organization's management and staff.

- Quadrant 4: High organizational readiness but low librarian readiness. Here, managers and staff of the organization may be pushing the library to develop an embedded model, but weaknesses among library staff are holding the library back.

To illustrate, first recall the readiness scores of the four scenarios:

- Scenario 1, Memorial Medical School and Hospital
  - Organizational readiness: −25
  - Librarian readiness: +47
- Scenario 2, Dewey, Cheatham, and Howe
  - Organizational readiness: −50
  - Librarian readiness: −18
- Scenario 3, Central Overshoe State University
  - Organizational readiness: +85
  - Librarian readiness: −30
- Scenario 4, Department of Justice
  - Organizational readiness: +100
  - Librarian readiness: +100

Keep in mind that the scores are not precise measurements. Think of them instead as broad indicators. What's of interest is the general position of the organization in one of the quadrants rather than the specific scores calculated.

In Scenario 1, the combination of negative organizational readiness (x-axis) and positive librarian readiness (y-axis) puts Memorial Medical School in Quadrant 2.

In Scenario 2, the combination of negative scores on both dimensions puts Dewey, Cheatham, and Howe in Quadrant 3.

In Scenario 3, Central Overshoe State falls into Quadrant 4 because of its combination of positive organizational readiness (x-axis) with negative librarian readiness (y-axis).

Finally, Scenario 4, the Department of Justice, with positive values on both librarian and organizational readiness, merits Quadrant 1.

Figure 7.2 shows the position of each organization on the readiness graph.

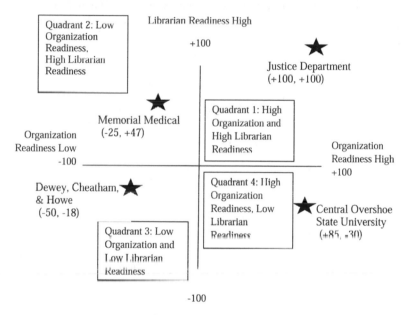

Figure 7.2   Position of Sample Scenarios on the Readiness Graph

Summary

This chapter explored frameworks for assessing the current status of embedded librarianship in an organization and the conditions contributing to or interfering with readiness to advance further. Both frameworks use a simple questionnaire that can be answered on behalf of an individual or an entire library staff, and in both questionnaires, factors are weighted to correspond roughly to research findings about the prevalence and importance of conditions among embedded librarians.

Scores on current status of embedded librarianship were translated into a series of stages, referred to as the Embedded Librarianship Maturity model.

The framework for assessing readiness to advance further consists of factors relating to the readiness of librarians and factors relating to the readiness of the parent organization to which the library belongs. A model was presented for visualizing readiness scores and grouping them into four categories, and this assessment and analysis process was illustrated with four scenarios.

Prepared with the understanding of the status and forces at work in their own context, librarians or library managers are now ready to move to the next step: developing a strategy for advancing embedded librarianship.

References

Machiavelli, N. 1952. *The prince*. New York: New American Library.

Shumaker, D., and M. Talley. 2009. *Models of embedded librarianship: Final report*. Alexandria, VA: Special Libraries Association.

Getting Started With Embedded Librarianship

Considering Your Options

Your organization is unique. Your strategy for embedded librarianship must be unique as well. Your uniqueness consists of many factors. You may be in a corporation, higher education, government, a nonprofit organization, primary or secondary education, or some other type of organization. Your organization may have tens of thousands of employees or only 10. Your library staff may be large, or you may be a solo librarian. You may have a large library building to administer or no physical collection and no space beyond an office or a cubicle. Your boss may be another librarian, an information technology manager, a facilities manager, the president of the company, or the leader of a specific information user group. The way that embedded librarianship is implemented and organized will depend on all of these factors and more.

The preceding chapter did not consider these factors. It assumed you could complete the exercises in a way that matched your situation. Your frame of reference could be yourself, as a solo librarian, or an entire library services department. The move from analysis to action, however, means it's time to explicitly recognize these differences. Here are three scenarios with which to begin:

- Combining centralized library services and embedded librarians in a single organization
- Separating centralized library services from embedded librarians
- Replacing centralized library services with embedded librarians

Combining Central Library and Embedded Operations

It's common in higher education, government agencies, large corporations, and other private-sector firms to have a centralized library of long standing. Managers and staff of these libraries are now looking for ways to reposition themselves as the role of the library changes and the value of traditional library services diminishes. One way to do that is to add embedded librarianship to the mix of functions that the library organization performs.

Combining centralized library operations with decentralized embedded librarianship raises complex issues of initiating and managing change. It also invites a review of the library's organizational structure. Too often, embedded roles are added to the duties of librarians without taking away other duties. There are numerous reports in the literature of reference and instruction librarians who become embedded in academic courses or corporate work groups but still share responsibility for reference duty or presenting one-shot instructional sessions. In the *Models of Embedded Librarianship* research project, 78.5 percent of respondents reported having a combination of specialized and general responsibilities (Shumaker and Talley, 2009). Often, the reality is that there is no alternative to combining the roles, at least in the early stages of embedded librarianship. On the other hand, there may be opportunities to separate the duties, especially if funding is provided by the group receiving the embedded librarian or by another source. In any case, the library manager should be aware of potential conflicts between the librarian's embedded role and general duties. Scheduling and task priority conflicts are bound to arise. On the other hand, perhaps the most robust organizational structure separates embedded librarians from general reference or reference-and-instruction librarians. In one unpublished case, the separation of the two functions enabled the embedded librarianship component of the library to grow severalfold over 4 years. In another case, the supervisor of library reference services also supervises embedded librarians, but the role and duties of the embedded librarians are distinct and do not include general services.

While the combination of embedded and centralized library operations increases complexity and raises questions for the library manager, it also may be the most desirable model for contributing the most valuable information to the organizational mission. Library units that follow this model often find synergies between the two that strengthen both of them.

The challenges and opportunities of coordinating embedded librarians and centralized library services are addressed in detail in Chapter 9.

Separating Centralized Library Services From Embedded Librarians

In some organizations, embedded librarians work independent of a centralized library and are under the direct supervision of the leader of the information user group in which they are embedded. In other cases, there may not be a centralized library at all. Of the respondents to the initial *Models of Embedded Librarianship* survey, 10 percent reported that there was no "library, information center, or similar information or knowledge services unit (such as a department)" within their organization (Shumaker and Talley, 2009). Some of these may be solo librarians, and I address their situation later in this chapter. There may be some librarians with embedded roles attached to the central library organization, while other librarians report to their information user groups and are administratively independent of the library.

Sometimes, internal circumstances may dictate that the library organization will not be able to administer embedded librarianship. These circumstances may be related to budget administration, lack of organizational experience with a matrixed organizational structure, or simple preferences of senior management. In these cases, the library manager's strategy for embedded librarianship will be to build an informal network—even advocating to leaders of groups that use information intensively that they hire their own librarians. The library manager can leverage this network to ensure that the central library is serving the organization effectively and can turn the embedded librarians into strong advocates for the library, while at the same time ensuring that the user groups that need specialized information and knowledge are able to obtain them in an optimal way.

Where there is a centralized library, and embedded librarians are independent of it, the relationship between the two can be synergistic or dysfunctional. The embedded librarians may be some of the heaviest users of the central library, both because they are used as go-betweens by other team members and by virtue of their embedded responsibilities. If communication and understanding between the two groups are poor, the central library staff may resent the embedded librarians and feel that they take credit for work done by the central staff. Meanwhile, the embedded librarians may feel the central library staff does not appreciate the needs of the organization.

Further, the embedded librarians may be isolated from one another and thus not able to develop or share tools and techniques that could benefit all. The library manager in this hybrid situation has an opportunity to build synergy by pursuing an informal network strategy. The manager can create opportunities for central library staff (embedded and not embedded) and independent embedded librarians to meet, get to know one another, share common problems and lessons learned, and identify and work on common solutions.

Replacing Centralized Library Services With Embedded Librarians

As noted in the previous section, a percentage of embedded librarians report that there is no centralized library operation in their organization. Some may be solo librarians; others may work alongside other embedded librarians in the same information user group or may have embedded colleagues working with other information user groups.

In some organizations, it may be that changes in the organization itself and changes in the nature of information use lead to the conclusion that a central library is no longer essential to the functioning of the organization. A highly decentralized management structure, heavy use of distributed teams and telework, and a highly dynamic, flexible environment frequently mark such situations. In these situations, the strategy for embedded librarianship is likely to involve a transition in which all librarians ultimately end up in embedded roles and the central library disappears as a physical and organizational entity. Davenport and Prusak (1993) advocated this eventuality in their article titled "Blow Up the Corporate Library," as did Judith Siess (2010).

Pursuing this strategy may be the most difficult option because it incorporates the greatest change—but it may be the only option in some cases, and the best for the organization in others. As part of the outcome, the librarians should seek to retain an informal network because there will be many matters of concern on which they will want to compare notes and develop common solutions. Ideally, this network should be recognized and even funded by the organization, so that the librarians will not have to "steal" time to participate in it.

Solo Librarians as Embedded Librarians

Are solo librarians embedded librarians? In the *Models of Embedded Librarianship* study, 12.5 percent of respondents in the initial survey reported that there was one and only one person in the organization providing library and information services. Of these respondents, 44 percent worked in organizations with fewer than 100 employees, and more than 75 percent worked in organizations with fewer than 500 employees. These solo librarians thus typically work in small organizations. I would speculate that they form close working relationships and take on a variety of duties, including some that are not traditionally associated with librarianship. They may find that there are certain individuals in the organization who call on them more than others do; solo librarians naturally become more engaged with the work of those individuals and form stronger working relationships with them than with others.

For these solo librarians, pursuing an embedded librarianship strategy is really a matter of finding the ways in which they can contribute the most to their organization and then doing those tasks. If maintaining a general library collection comes into conflict with working closely with a group on a strategically important project, the librarian needs to either hand off the lower-value tasks or discontinue them entirely. On the positive side, because of the informality of many small organizations, these librarians often have opportunities to demonstrate what they can do and to break down any lingering stereotypes about the roles and limitations of librarians. An embedded role may well be the cornerstone, or the entirety, of the strategy for these solo librarians to strengthen their value to the organization.

A Framework for Action Planning

Embedded librarianship initiatives, like any other initiatives, can and do fail. Therefore, it's important to first assess conditions. If some conditions in the environment are not favorable, then it will be necessary to change them before taking direct action on the initiative. Chapter 7 discussed assessing the current status of embedded librarianship in an organization and the readiness for starting or expanding the embedded model. It also illustrated the assessment process and outcomes with four scenarios.

Armed with their assessment, and having explored the options for organizing and managing embedded librarianship, librarians can now translate the assessment into actions. Here are four broad strategies, corresponding to the quadrants on the readiness graph in Chapter 7 and illustrated with the four scenarios from that chapter:

- Quadrant 1: High organizational and high librarian readiness
  - Strategy: Implement embedded librarianship as a strategic priority.
  - Case study: Department of Justice
- Quadrant 2: Low organizational readiness but high librarian readiness
  - Strategy: Empower library staff and build organizational readiness.
  - Case study: Memorial Medical School and Hospital library
- Quadrant 3: Low organizational readiness and low librarian readiness
  - Strategy: Begin to lay the groundwork.
  - Case study: Dewey, Cheatham, and Howe
- Quadrant 4: High organizational readiness, but low librarian readiness
  - Strategy: Develop and engage library staff to seize the opportunities.
  - Case study: Central Overshoe State University

Figure 8.1 depicts these strategy options.

Each of the quadrants poses a different challenge for the library manager who wants to initiate embedded librarianship. What's most significant is that in three of the four scenarios, the time is not ripe to implement the embedded model. Preliminary work must be done first. Quadrant 1 is the exception: with few obstacles in the way, the Justice Department library manager can initiate embedded librarianship in the near future.

Considering each option in turn, I'll leave Quadrant 1 for last, and start with a discussion of the preparatory work needed in the other three scenarios.

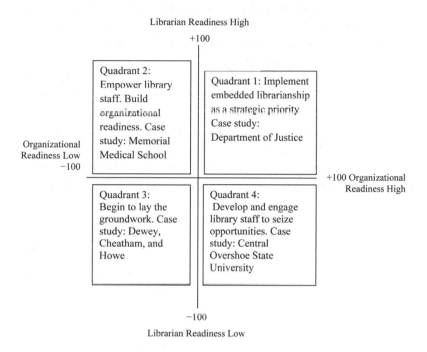

Figure 8.1   Four Strategy Options

Quadrant 2 Strategy: Empower Library Staff, Build Organizational Readiness

If you are in Quadrant 2, like Memorial Medical, the librarians have a positive mix of skills, knowledge of the domain and context, and motivation to seek embedded roles, but conditions in the organization are not favorable. Thus, the first priority must be to change those conditions. How to do that? Two ways that have proven effective in diverse organizations are volunteering and outreach initiatives both to managers of key information user groups and to senior managers in the library's own hierarchy.

Any and all opportunities to volunteer in the workplace are potentially valuable. Whether it is a corporate charity activity, sports team, employee club, or something more work-related, any volunteer group enables librarians to get to know employees from other units. Of equal importance for a Quadrant 2 strategy, librarians' volunteering enables those other employees to get to know the librarians. It breaks down functional and administrative barriers in the organization and ties the librarians into the office grapevine. It also gives the librarians the chance to show that they can contribute—and combats misconceptions that they are merely clerical employees with limited skills. If the volunteer opportunity is work-related, the payoff may be even greater. In one case, a newly hired librarian in an academic institution asked to join a curriculum review committee. Thanks to her influence, a recommendation for the inclusion of embedded librarians in courses emerged as one of the committee's proposals.

All library staff members, especially reference staff, can volunteer. In the case of Memorial Medical, the enthusiasm of the reference librarians can be channeled into seeking relationship-building volunteer activities.

On the other hand, management outreach may require the library manager to take the lead. In most cases, the library manager's supervisor will be the first stop. Upper management support can open doors and facilitate progress. Only in unusual circumstances in which the managers in the library's reporting chain are immovable obstacles to progress might it be necessary to proceed without involving them. A decision to do that is risky and should not be undertaken lightly.

Once the library's management hierarchy is informed, the outreach initiative can proceed to holding exploratory meetings with leaders of information user groups. First, the librarians have to identify information user-group leaders who will be receptive to a meeting request. In some organizations, some managers may ignore such requests. The librarians should meet with whomever they can—ideally, leaders who are known as having high promotion potential and who are leading groups that are well-respected and engaged in important corporate strategic initiatives. The library manager might go alone to this kind of meeting, or a librarian who has done some work for the group might attend as well. Although the Quadrant 2 categorization suggests that organizational relationships are weak, it is still possible that a member of the library staff has already formed a relationship with one or more members of the information user group. If so, the outreach meeting should take advantage of it.

The focus of this kind of outreach meeting should not be to promote embedded librarianship. That may be too exotic a concept to bring up this early in the process. It also presumes that the information user group should have an embedded librarian. To take that approach is to make the classic marketing mistake of promoting what you have, instead of first understanding the needs of your audience. The outreach meeting should focus on the information user group. Afterward, the librarians can begin to align products and services to meet their needs. The message should be that the librarians want to understand the information user group better so that they can improve their responsiveness to its needs. The information user-group manager may or may not think that better support is needed from the library. The librarians may be able to address a lack of interest by citing work that library staff members have done for members of the group. It's possible that the manager of the group is unaware of these contributions. Stories may get the group manager thinking about the possibilities. As the group manager becomes engaged, the librarians should look for openings to set up follow-up activities. The group manager may suggest that they meet with members of the group. There may be an invitation to attend a group meeting, perhaps even to attend on a regular basis, just to gain more understanding of the group's work. If such an invitation is not forthcoming, the librarians should suggest it, just on a trial basis.

If a meeting of this type goes well, the librarians will leave with follow-up actions that can lead to further relationship building. They will have "gotten their foot in the door," to use the old description of door-to-door sales tactics. Eventually, they may achieve the level of trust and mutual commitment that characterizes a strong embedded relationship. On the other hand, the meeting may not yield such positive results. Perhaps the group's work is such that a deeper involvement of the librarians does not seem productive at this time. Perhaps the group manager is simply not responsive. If those are the outcomes, so be it. The librarians should cross that group off their list for the time being and move on to other prospects that hold greater chances of success.

Quadrant 4 Strategy: Develop and Engage Library Staff, Seize the Opportunities

Quadrant 4, represented by Central Overshoe State University, has the opposite problem from Memorial Medical in Quadrant 2. Managers and staff in the information user community are demanding to involve librarians more closely in their work, but the readiness of librarians is weak. In this case, the library manager must do two things: help the librarians to develop, and manage user expectations so that the present opportunity is not lost.

To help the librarians develop, the library manager must take a closer look at the specific areas in which the librarians are weak. If there are professional development needs in the areas of research and analysis, instructional design and delivery, or content management, there are many ways to meet them. The options range from formal academic coursework to webinars offered by professional associations and vendors and to on-the-job practice and experimentation. If the development needs lie in the areas of subject domain knowledge, the options are similar. The organization may offer in-house training courses that the librarians can enroll in, or formal academic coursework may be appropriate. If the need is a greater understanding of organizational context, the library manager should explore whether there are orientation programs in which the librarians could join. In one professional services firm, newly hired librarians participate in the same in-depth orientation series as other professionals, thereby gaining the same perspective on the firm that other professionals have. Finally, the volunteering strategy that can be valuable for outreach in a Quadrant 2 initiative can also be an opportunity for librarians in a Quadrant 4 situation to learn more about the organization, simply by meeting, talking with, and forming relationships with employees from other groups.

If, however, the areas of readiness in which librarians are weak happen to be the capability and motivation to participate in outreach and form working relationships, then the library manager will have to take different steps. These steps are likely to be very dependent on the needs of each librarian and to involve some combination of confidence building and motivation on both the group and the individual level.

Some librarians may think of themselves as introverts. They may also think that as introverts, they are not capable of marketing, promoting, or selling their services. They may indeed score high for introversion on the Myers-Briggs or other personality tests. Even so, this does not mean they are incapable of developing the working relationships necessary to perform effectively or of becoming embedded librarians. There are many examples of successful embedded librarians who consider themselves to be introverts. The librarian who uses introversion as an excuse to avoid outreach may need individual counseling and support to understand that being an introvert does not preclude initiating relationships. Suggest specific techniques to break the ice and get involved.

The library manager may need to employ a range of motivational tactics. There is not room in this chapter for a full discussion of motivational techniques, but a few observations may illustrate major options. Lack of motivation could be related to fear or complacency. If the former, the library manager may need to be supportive while the librarian takes small steps that build confidence. Using a "buddy" or mentoring approach may help a junior librarian gain confidence. If the latter, the library manager may need to lay out the case that the options open to the library, and to the individual, are to change or to become irrelevant. Job descriptions may need to be changed, and the librarians given the choice of performing to new expectations or experiencing negative consequences. Local circumstances and rules will govern how this change can be accomplished. In one case, a library manager met individually with several librarians whose duties would be affected by the change to embedded librarianship. The manager helped them to see the necessity of the change and to adapt to its new requirements. In another case, a librarian who was successful in developing an embedded role was made the supervisor of a reference team, putting her into a position in which she could motivate them, mentor them, and help them make the transition from traditional reference work to embedded roles.

The library manager dealing with relationship-building capability and motivational issues may wish to adopt ideas from the literature on interpersonal communication, change management, and supervision. Here are a few helpful books:

- *Crucial Conversations: Tools for Talking When Stakes Are High*, by Kerry Patterson, et al.
- *Influencer: The Power to Change Anything*, by Kerry Patterson, et al.
- *Leading Change*, by John P. Kotter
- *Managing Transitions: Making the Most of Change*, by William Bridges

Meanwhile, the library manager in a Quadrant 4 situation also has the challenge of managing the expectations of information users who are eager to incorporate an embedded librarian into their plans.

Managing expectations is a delicate balancing act. On one hand, the library manager needs to be positive and responsive to the demand, to adopt a can-do attitude. On the other hand, the manager must ensure that the information users do not expect more, and faster, response than can be delivered. If they become disappointed, the prospects for embedded librarianship and the manager's own position may be jeopardized. One strategy is to look for initial actions—baby steps—that can be taken to address some of the users' needs and to develop toward a fully embedded model. In the case of Central Overshoe State University, the librarians are new and inexperienced but presumably willing to take on an innovative role. Perhaps one or two of them would like to take on a limited role in a course—or perhaps share it, so that they could support each other. With enthusiasm for the opportunity, they may be willing to take on extra work in the short run, while the library manager works on filling the current vacancies.

Meanwhile, the library manager should be candid with the information user group—in this case, the faculty members—about the library's limitations and call on them for help in working with the librarians to develop their capabilities. The library manager's plans to address the limitations must also be part of the message. In the Central Overshoe State example, the library manager needs to propose what the library can do today, why there are present limitations, and what is being done to address those limitations and enable the library to respond more fully in the future.

Quadrant 3 Strategy: Begin to Lay the Groundwork

In Quadrant 3, both librarian readiness and organizational readiness are negative. It would seem that there are no prospects for the establishment of embedded librarianship. The library manager in this situation will require patience and a combination of Quadrant 2 and Quadrant 4 strategies.

The library manager can start by looking closely at the elements of the readiness questionnaire. If there are a few relatively strong elements to build on, such as a few respected regular users of the library or members of the library staff who have the potential to form strong working relationships, then the manager can begin slowly to develop the conditions for embedded librarianship. In the case of Dewey, Cheatham, and Howe, the senior librarian can initiate outreach meetings with the few partners who use the library regularly, to explore their needs and perhaps introduce the idea of building up library services over time. The senior librarian can also begin to discuss the future with the junior librarian and motivate the junior librarian to take part in the outreach work. It will take time, so the manager should persist, using ideas from the Quadrant 2 and Quadrant 4 strategies and looking for opportunities to advance the case. As the situation progresses, the status of factors may change, so the manager should reassess readiness from time to time and adjust the strategy as appropriate. If all goes well, the manager's efforts will be rewarded— eventually.

Quadrant 1 Strategy: Implement Embedded Librarianship

If you find yourself solidly in Quadrant 1, as in the Department of Justice scenario, then there are few if any obstacles in the way of implementing embedded librarianship. Library staff members have the skills and motivation, as well as the organizational and subject domain knowledge, needed to succeed. Key managers, ideally at all levels of the organization, are already fans of the librarians, willing to support an initiative to increase the value of the librarians to the organization, and there are pockets of demonstrated need for in-depth collaboration between librarians and other professionals—illustrated by the presence of influential library users.

The Department of Justice case study describes the best of all possible worlds. It remains necessary only to work out the details. Of course, these details can be significant. The library director will have two primary tasks: to establish a solid foundation for a successful embedded relationship and to plan for the transition.

Although the actions needed to sustain the new model and evaluate it over time are detailed in Chapters 9 and 10, the library director needs to think about them at the beginning of the process. Briefly, it is important to clarify what expectations the information users have of the library organization. It is just as important to document what expectations the library manager and the soon-to-be-embedded librarian have of the information user group. What actions will the information user-group manager commit to in order to build and sustain the relationship? Many promising partnerships have foundered on the rocks of assumptions about shared commitments that really were not shared. Although it isn't common practice, documenting the arrangement can be a good idea. Even an exchange of emails confirming the outlines of responsibilities and expectations can be useful. But whether the terms of engagement are documented formally or not, it's important to discuss them and be sure they are clear.

In planning the transition, the library director's focus will be on the ripple effects of reassigning even one librarian to an embedded role.

First, what will happen to centralized library services formerly performed by the newly embedded staff? Will more staff be hired to backfill reference duty or other tasks the embedded librarians can no longer perform? If not, will other staff be reassigned to do them, or will those tasks no longer be required? These questions are not likely to concern the information user-group managers, such as the section chief and division director in our Justice Department example. Instead, the library director will need to work out answers.

Next, how will the change be communicated to the information users and the library staff? The library director may assume that the section chief will explain the change to the attorneys in the section, but it's wise to make this expectation clear. At the same time, the library director will need to communicate with all library staff.

Negative Factors in Quadrant 1 Situations

In real life, few situations are so uniformly positive as the Justice Department case study. Even if the overall readiness assessment places the organization into the first quadrant, there are likely to be countervailing factors—weak areas or soft spots in readiness—that the library director must take into account. Library staff members are likely to vary in their readiness, for reasons of either librarianship skills, subject and context understanding, or motivation. Managers and members of information user groups too are likely to vary in their openness to collaboration. A common complaint among librarians in higher education, for example, is that faculty members resist yielding class time to a librarian to present information literacy instruction.

The presence of negative factors in a generally positive Quadrant 1 scenario leads to two imperatives for management action. The first is to remediate the soft spots in the overall picture. The second is to take care in selecting the information user-group partner and librarian for an initial embedded engagement. To remediate soft spots, the library manager can adopt relevant ideas from Quadrant 2 and 4 scenarios. As for selecting the right opportunity, there are several considerations in deciding what that is.

The first point is that an "all at once" strategy is unlikely to succeed. Because librarians are at different stages of readiness and information user groups vary in their receptiveness to the embedded model, a decision by library management that all reference librarians shall go forth and become embedded is likely to have a few different results:

- With luck, some librarians will be successful in establishing strong relationships, will prove their value, and will continue as embedded librarians. But almost certainly, some will not. Their relationships will not develop the necessary levels of trust and close collaboration, and they will backslide to old reference work.

- Some librarians may leave the organization. They may conclude that they no longer fit in the organization and seek other employment.

- Some information user groups may be disillusioned by their negative experiences and become less likely to be receptive to future embedded librarianship initiatives.

Clearly, the stakes are high. Because an "all at once" strategy carries these risks, the library manager may want to consider a phased approach or a pilot program that can be scaled up over time.

With the adoption of a pilot approach, the next decision becomes which opportunities to start with. Which librarian, which information user group, which engagement will be the most promising pilot program? The Justice Department scenario provides some answers. The proposed engagement appears to have all the ingredients for success. It includes a highly professional librarian who is ready and eager to take on an embedded role and a strongly supportive, well-respected information user group. It has strong senior management support, as well. With these advantages, there is a high probability of success. There is also the expectation that the success will be visible—to other midlevel and senior managers, as well as to other librarians. In short, the proposed embedded relationship is likely to result in a short-term success story that will serve as a model to both other information user groups and other librarians. In the best case, other information user-group managers will beat a path to the library manager's door, requesting that their group get "one of those" embedded librarians as well. In the worst case, the library manager will have an example to use in persuading other information user groups to engage an embedded librarian.

A Framework for Analyzing Opportunities

Starting with a pilot program and scaling up may be a better strategy for embedded librarianship in many organizations than an all-at-once library services revolution. The successful pilot will provide a model that can be communicated throughout the organization and replicated for new information user groups. However, selecting the right opportunities becomes a critical factor in the plan. The best pilot program is one that is important, involves a respected partner, and is successful. To determine the importance of a candidate project, the library manager needs to understand the strategy of the parent organization. Figure 8.2 presents a worksheet for analyzing opportunities in terms of the organization's strategic priorities.

The ideal candidate project is one that addresses a problem that is strategically important to the organization. It offers the opportunity for an embedded librarian to make a significant contribution and involves information user organizations in which librarians are already providing support and forming good working relationships.

Following are four new scenarios. To illustrate the analysis of strategic opportunities for embedded librarianship, each scenario is accompanied by an analysis of the ways that an embedded librarian could contribute to achieving the organization's strategic goal.

Scenario 1

At Ginormous State University, the faculty and administration have decided to focus on "learning how to learn"—incorporating the development of research and writing assignments into a new series of interdisciplinary seminars that will be required of first-year and advanced students.

Analysis: Here is a great opportunity for the librarians. The initiative is a university priority. The librarians' expertise in teaching information literacy should be a vital contribution to it. Ideally, the librarians should

Organization Mission, Goal, or Objective	Library Role: Current/Potential	Opportunity for Embedded Library Services

Figure 8.2   Strategic Opportunity Analysis Worksheet

already be part of the planning and development team. If not, they should use their campus relationships to get involved. Pre-existing relationships with respected members of the team would be valuable for this purpose.

Scenario 2

At the firm of Wise Consultants, the number of management consulting engagements has recently increased, and the firm has hired a number of new junior staff. While the partners and employees are happy that business is good, senior partners are concerned about maintaining the quality of the firm's work, given the relative inexperience of the new staff. At the same time, the library is experiencing an increase in reference requests, and often it happens that different librarians are receiving the same or similar requests from different members of a single consulting team.

Analysis: The strategic problem of maintaining quality during an expansion of the business is a multidimensional one, and the librarians can offer only one element of a solution. Establishing embedded relationships in the consulting teams would certainly help manage the demand on librarians better, but that's not the strategic problem from the firm's point of view.

In proposing embedded librarianship, the librarians need to consider how they can help share expertise across the firm. One option might be to make embedded librarians the stewards of a shared knowledge repository. They could ensure that key documents from each engagement were contributed and might even capture "lessons learned" at the end of each project. A pilot project to establish such a repository for a respected practice group would be a way to test the concept and, if successful, build a prototype that could be extended.

Scenario 3

The National Patent Agency is responsible for reviewing patent applications and deciding whether to grant a patent or not. Its leaders recognize the importance of information in its operations. Patent examiners, who specialize in particular technical disciplines, must determine whether an application represents a truly novel development or has already been documented in prior patents or technical literature. The agency's leaders need to overcome two problems: New patent examiners are not aware of the technical literature resources at their disposal, and experienced examiners do not keep current with developments in the literature sources.

Analysis: The agency offers another example of an important problem to which librarians can be a key part of the solution. Adding embedded librarians to the patent examiner groups would address both the continuing education needs of the veteran examiners and the need for training new examiners.

The librarians can select an examiner group to join forces on a pilot program that could be a model for the agency. The ideal partner group would be well-run, highly regarded, and one with which the librarians already have good relationships.

Scenario 4

Metropolitan Hospital is a busy urban facility. Because of the fast pace, doctors and nurses rarely consult the medical literature for insights to aid in their diagnostic and treatment decisions. Senior leaders of the hospital are concerned about the possibility of medical errors and would like the literature to be used more effectively.

Analysis: Here, the strategic initiative is to ensure that diagnosis and treatment are based on the best available evidence from the literature. Embedded informationists could be the solution. A pilot program involving a respected department could demonstrate the value of the informationist and serve as a model for rollout to other groups.

Matching Actions to Readiness

For the four scenarios analyzed in Chapter 7, the following exercise presents a list of actions that a library manager could take to advance the goal of implementing embedded librarianship. In some cases, an action may be appropriate to more than one scenario. Match the actions to the scenario(s) for which they would be appropriate. Following this exercise is a suggested solution.

Action Planning Exercise

Referring to the four Readiness Scenarios introduced in Chapter 7, which actions from the following list would be appropriate in each scenario? Why?

Scenario	Quadrant	Actions
1. Memorial Medical School and Hospital	2	
2. Dewey, Cheatham, and Howe	3	
3. Central Overshoe State University	4	
4. Department of Justice	1	

Actions

A. Senior librarian/library director proposes to boss that she volunteer to join a new Strategic Planning Committee that is being formed.

B. Librarians join a staff recreation committee.

C. Librarians learn about the organization by participating in staff orientation programs designed for newly hired doctors/lawyers/faculty.

D. Librarian proposes to boss a plan to meet with managers of key information user groups to propose having a librarian attend each group's staff meetings.

E. Library director asks library staff members to make a list of their best, most frequent, most supportive information users. Director holds a brainstorming session with staff about ways to reach out to these users and the groups where they work.

F. Library staff members are encouraged to attend workshops and conferences related to the work of the organization.

G. Senior librarian or library director negotiates with the leaders of key information user groups and assesses staffing impacts of embedded librarianship within the library organization.

H. Senior librarian or library director holds group meetings at which a change to embedded librarianship is discussed and meets with library staff members individually to discuss the impact of such a change on them.

Memorial Medical School and Hospital (Quadrant 2)

Because the emphasis is on empowering library staff and building organizational readiness, actions A, B, D, and E would be the highest priorities.

Actions A and B will help raise the visibility of the library staff to others in the organization and lead to the formation of management and employee relationships that may help identify opportunities for the future. Action D is the kind of preliminary outreach that may lead directly to new working relationships, while action E prepares the way for action D by enlisting the librarians in developing a list of potential target groups for the outreach effort.

Dewey, Cheatham, and Howe (Quadrant 3)

Quadrant 3 organizations have few resources on which to build in the near term. The most feasible actions might be A, B, C, and F. Actions B, C, and F are aimed at increasing the new, inexperienced librarian's understanding of the subject domains and political context of the organization. Action B will have the added benefit of making the librarian more visible and better connected with other employees. Action A will give the library director an opportunity to build management relationships, gain insights into organizational strategic priorities, and perhaps identify initial opportunities for the library to contribute.

Central Overshoe State University (Quadrant 4)

In Quadrant 4, the priority is to develop and engage staff to seize the present opportunities. The most likely actions would be B, C, F, H, and perhaps G. As in the Quadrant 3 strategy, actions B, C, and F are calculated to increase the subject domain and political context awareness of the staff. Action H is important to present the proposed change, discuss the opportunities and the ramifications of failing to change, and begin the change process for each staff member. Action G would be appropriate if the library director believes that some initial steps can be taken in the near future.

Department of Justice (Quadrant 1)

The Department of Justice, in Quadrant 1, is ready to initiate embedded librarianship. Therefore, action G, and perhaps H, are the most directly applicable. Action G is required to implement the embedded model. Action H may be redundant if staff are already prepared for the change, but it would be important if some staff members are unclear about it or resistant to a new model.

Developing Your Action Plan

This chapter has translated the readiness assessments from Chapter 7 into ideas for action. It has identified actions that are geared to particular readiness conditions. By reflecting on and analyzing the factors in your situation, you can follow the same process to build your own action plan.

As you do this, you may wish to make systematic notes of your plan; it is recommended that you do so. If you're familiar with project planning methods and a planning tool, you may wish to use it to manage your plan. If you don't have, or don't wish to use, a planning tool, the simple template provided by Figure 8.3 can be used for this purpose.

For each action you plan to take, you should describe what you expect to gain. This step will help ensure clarity about the importance of proposed tasks and enable you to review the outcomes later. You should also establish an expected date of completion. As Duke Ellington is said to have remarked, "I don't need time, I need a deadline!" So give yourself a

Action	Outcomes Expected	Completion Date
1.		
2.		
3.		
4.		
5.		
6.		
7.		
8.		
9.		
10.		

Figure 8.3   Action Planning Template

deadline. Finally, if you list an action for which you can't specify an outcome or a target date, that action is probably too vague and too broad. In that case, break it down to more specific actions with their own outcomes and dates. It's fine to nest your actions in a hierarchy.

As you complete your plan and begin to carry it out, it's good to start planning for success. How will you sustain embedded librarianship over time? That's the subject of the next chapter.

Summary

Chapter 8 analyzed the different organizational models for embedded librarianship. It contrasted the option of managing embedded librarians and a centralized library operation under one organizational umbrella with the option placing embedded librarians under the direct supervision of information user-group managers, with or without a separate central library services operation.

It then turned to translating the results of Chapter 7's readiness assessment into an action plan for initiating or extending embedded librarianship. The readiness assessment shows which aspects of the environment are favorable to the change and which may need to be addressed before the change can proceed. It examined four scenarios in turn, concluding with the scenario in which all considerations are favorable and the change can be introduced. It ended with ideas for introducing embedded librarianship to the organization.

References

Davenport, T. H., and L. Prusak. 1993. Blow up the corporate library. *International Journal of Information Management* 13: 405–412.

Shumaker, D., and M. Talley. 2009. *Models of embedded librarianship: Final report.* Alexandria, VA: Special Libraries Association.

Siess, J. 2010. Embedded librarianship. *Searcher* 18 (1): 38–45.

Chapter 9

Sustaining Your Embedded Role

It's important to have a successful beginning in an embedded librarianship program, but it isn't the whole job. Success requires sustained and prolonged management attention. If management engagement falters, the initial success will slip away. Library managers have two kinds of sustaining responsibilities. They take routine actions to tend embedded relationships and intervene to prevent or fix problems that crop up. This chapter addresses both kinds of responsibilities. It introduces the four habits of successful embedded librarians, relates some of the problems and pitfalls, and suggests what you can do about them.

The Habits of Successful Embedded Librarians

In their study *Models of Embedded Librarianship*, Shumaker and Talley (2009) found a number of practices that differentiate successful embedded librarians from less-successful embedded librarians. They grouped these practices into four broad themes:

1. Marketing and promotion
2. Delivery of sophisticated, value-added services
3. Ongoing service evaluation and communication of the evaluation results
4. Engagement and support of library and information user-group management

A subsequent reanalysis of the data, using different criteria for success, found broad support for these themes, although specific factors and practices varied with the criteria used (Shumaker, 2011b). Chapter 10 addresses evaluation, and the other three themes are discussed here.

Habit 1: Marketing and Promotion

Successful embedded librarians publicize what they are doing. Academic librarians put a page and a sign-up form on their websites so that faculty members can request to have an embedded librarian assigned to their courses. They email instructors before each term, reminding them that embedded librarians are available to consult on research assignments, teach information literacy and research skills, and act as research counselors to students. Corporate librarians make presentations at employee orientations and at "all hands" staff meetings or place articles about embedded librarians and their work in employee magazines. The list of potential media is limited only by your imagination. The point is to choose the media that will communicate most effectively in your environment.

For example, the idea of presenting at new employee orientations is controversial. On one hand, the extended analysis published by Shumaker (2011b) found that this was the only specific form of promotion that distinguished the most successful embedded librarians from others, no matter what definition of success was used. On the other hand, some librarians are skeptical of its value. There are several reasons for their skepticism. First, new employee orientations are often rushed affairs, jam-packed with administrative information and forms to fill out to register for benefits and the like. The librarians are crowded into a time slot that is much too short. Second, depending on the timing of the new employee orientation session, it may not coincide with an actual need on the part of the employee. New employees often take some time to settle into their work and begin to be productive. If the orientation session is too early, the employees will not be able to relate the librarian's presentation to their needs. Because memories that are not put into a meaningful context fade quickly, by the time they progress far enough in their work that they could use the librarians' assistance, they may have forgotten about the information they received at the new-employee orientation.

The importance of word-of-mouth publicity should not be overlooked. The initial *Models of Embedded Librarianship* analysis found it to be a statistically significant differentiator of successful programs (Shumaker and Talley, 2009). While its significance was not confirmed in the subsequent analysis, anecdotes from embedded librarians often mention the importance of word-of-mouth recommendations by professionals with whom they have worked. In one case, reported in a follow-up to the *Models of Embedded Librarianship* research, a university faculty member said that her comments on the success of her partnership with an embedded

librarian "created great jealousy" among her colleagues in other departments (Shumaker, 2011a, Site Visit 5). This is why you should select partners who are well-respected when initiating your first embedded
librarianship pilot program. The testimonials of a manager and staff who
are well-respected by their peers may be worth far more than all the self-
promotion a library staff could possibly generate.

The central point is that embedded librarians (all librarians, really)
should have a communications strategy and a plan. The following steps
will help you formulate your plan.

Start with the groups you are trying to reach and the media that will
reach them. Who are the decision makers? For example, in an academic
institution, the students are the ultimate beneficiaries of embedded information literacy instruction because it helps them become better learners
and, ultimately, more-successful professionals as they progress through
their careers. But the students are not the decision makers—it's the
instructors who decide whether a course will have an embedded librarian.
Indeed, it may not be the individual instructor who decides, but a course
chair or curriculum development group. How will you reach those influ-
encers and decision makers? What media will they see and pay attention
to? There are many options available to you. Which will be most effective?
In this context, participating in task forces and planning groups can be
seen as a marketing communication opportunity. However, the participation must be genuinely focused on contributing to the group, or it will ultimately be seen as inauthentic and probably unconvincing.

Then, define your message. What message will catch the attention of
each audience you identified? Most likely, it will be some variation on the
theme that an embedded librarian can make the lives of others in the
organization (faculty, marketers, researchers, administrators) easier and
more successful. In any case, emphasize the benefits to the audience—the
"What's In It For Me" (WIIFM) principle. In crafting the message, take
advantage of the power of word of mouth: Use testimonials from delighted
and well-respected partners to help make your point.

Finally, include timing in your planning. It's critical. For example, the
time to approach instructors about embedded instruction is not the first
week of classes for the academic term—it's earlier than that, when they are
planning the content, assignments, and schedules. In a corporate
research and development organization, there may be an internal
research and development grant process, in which researchers compete
for internally funded grants to pursue their ideas. The library manager

would want to reach those researchers at least twice—when they are preparing their budgets, to ensure that information and knowledge contributions of embedded librarians are included, and immediately after awards are made, to highlight the availability and value of embedded librarians.

Figure 9.1 presents a simple template that can be used for communications planning.

Habit 2: Sophisticated, Value-Added Work Contributions

The second habit of successful embedded librarians is the ability to make sophisticated, complex, value-added contributions to the work of the

Target Audience and Media	Message	Timing
1.		
2.		
3.		
4.		
5.		
6.		
7.		
8.		
9.		
10.		

Figure 9.1   Communications Planning Worksheet

partner group. The nature of those contributions varies with the needs of the group. Librarians develop different areas of expertise in information management, any of which may be relevant to a particular group. As shown in Chapter 3, the primary type of contribution in higher education has been the teaching of information literacy skills, which contributes to the educational mission of the university. In corporate and other special-ized settings, the nature of the contribution may be performing in-depth topical research and analysis; highly focused news alerting; creating and maintaining a taxonomy for a team's internal documentation; or building and maintaining a database, an intranet site, or an externally facing web-site. All of these, and more, are within the librarian's purview. The impor-tant point is that the contribution matches the needs of the organization. It must be highly professional and valued.

With all this emphasis on complex, sophisticated, value-added work, some readers may wonder what happens to the more traditional types of work performed by librarians—bibliographic citation checking, docu-ment delivery, and the like. The fact is, embedded librarianship doesn't make these tasks go away. Instead, think of the complex, value-added work as layered on top of, or built upon, the foundation of these basic tasks. In the *Models of Embedded Librarianship* research, 92 percent of the embedded librarians reported that they perform "ready reference" work—in fact, it was the most common task performed, given all the options in the survey. Just under half said they performed document delivery tasks. In fact, the initial analysis of factors that differentiated suc-cessful embedded librarians found that the successful librarians were actually more likely to perform document delivery than the less success-ful (Shumaker and Talley, 2009). This distinction was not confirmed in the extended analysis. Still, librarians and their managers should not assume that all traditional functions will disappear when embedded librarianship is established. Some of them, such as ready reference and document delivery, could be performed by the embedded librarian or referred to support staff. Either way, these traditional functions continue to provide a necessary infrastructure for more-complex work.

It's important, also, to define what distinguishes the highly valued work of the embedded librarian from traditional library services. After all, librarians have long done bibliographic instruction without being embed-ded. They have done in-depth research, current awareness, and catego-rization of information, all without being embedded.

Value must be measured from the information user's point of view. The librarian's ability to deliver value ultimately derives from the combination of the librarian's skills with the depth and duration of the relationship itself. For example, the dominant mode of information literacy instruction in U.S. higher education has been the one-shot instruction session. A class visits the library, or a librarian visits a classroom, during one class period for a lecture and orientation about the use of the library and its services. Period.

The brief nature of the encounter between librarian and students automatically limits its value. The librarian has limited knowledge of the course topic or requirements. The students get little opportunity to assess their skills, practice the application of new concepts, or confirm their progress. Similarly, the research librarian who has limited contact with a research team can only deliver search results that are a rough approximation of what the team needs. The team would be foolish to trust a librarian who is little better than a casual acquaintance with sophisticated decisions about relevance and importance, no matter how advanced the librarian's professional skills. Further, because information overload has become so acute in the current age of information abundance, the librarian who cannot be trusted to analyze information and data, and provide a highly distilled product, is more of a hindrance than a help and thus will be avoided.

It's the librarian who enjoys a strong working relationship with the information user group who is able to overcome this problem. The *Models of Embedded Librarianship* research indicated that many embedded librarians did not have extensive experience or formal education in the subject field of the information user group before initiating their embedded role (Shumaker and Talley, 2009). However, they develop it—often rapidly—and sometimes end up as domain experts themselves. For example, Shumaker and Talley interviewed an embedded librarian who, after a period of years working in a specific domain, has served on national and international industry and technical standards bodies.

One more point about sustaining the delivery of value-added services: The definition of *value added* is constantly changing, meaning the nature of the librarian's work must change as well. This point echoes the thinking of some of the management writers mentioned in Chapter 2, particularly Friedman and Pink. What can be automated, will be automated. What can be outsourced, or "offshored," will be. More and more functions that are exclusively left-brain by nature are susceptible to these trends. Librarians must move up the value chain—embedded librarians in particular.

Successful embedded librarians move up the value chain relentlessly. In an organization studied by Shumaker, an embedded librarian produced a specialized news alert for several years, manually selecting stories to be included. At first, the librarian consulted the information user-group manager on every story included, to confirm the librarian's judgment about what was important. Later, the librarian was trusted to make almost all judgments unilaterally. Then, new tools became available to help automate the selection process and reduce the amount of the librarian's time needed to produce the news alert. By adopting them, with the guidance and leadership of the library manager, the librarian was able to devote more time to other tasks critical to the progress of the information user group (Shumaker, 2011a).

In an academic organization, librarians have experimented with different embedded models of information literacy instruction, migrating from customized, individualized responses to reliance on prepared, off-the-shelf answers for the most common queries and to the development of online, self-paced tutorials with pre- and posttests to assess progress. Along the way, librarians have become core team members in the university's curriculum development process so that they are better able to influence the incorporation of information literacy learning objectives and instruction into the most appropriate areas of the curriculum in a consistent manner. They have moved up the value chain (Shumaker, 2011a).

There is another important subtheme to this need to evolve. Sometimes, particularly when a task is repetitive, as in the production of a news alert, and is handed off from the embedded librarian who created it to a successor or another staff member, it loses its edge—and thereby its value. The objective subtly shifts from ensuring that the critical information needs of the user group are met to producing the next issue of the news alert. The relationship atrophies, the person responsible for the product or services does not have the same intuitive grasp of the need, and the value is lost. When this happens, it's likely that sooner or later the user-group manager will reassess the embedded librarian's role, conclude that it is no longer fulfilling its purpose, and end it. The embedded librarian and the library manager must proactively monitor and assess the status of the work being done and monitor the health of the relationship.

Habit 3: Management Engagement and Support

The final point of the preceding section leads directly into the third habit of successful embedded librarians. They leverage the engagement of both information user-group management and library management. This principle reinforces the point made in Chapter 7 that embedded librarianship requires a partnership at the management level. It also underlines the point that library managers must lead the transition from the front. They cannot push the librarians out of the library door while they stay behind in their offices.

As noted in Chapter 8, it is important to articulate the information user-group manager's commitment to the embedded librarian at the time the relationship is established. Any partnership must be reciprocal. Information user-group managers can demonstrate their commitment to the partnership by any of a number of actions. The actions they take are driven largely by the organizational context. Some of the common actions are listed here:

- Funding the embedded librarian, in whole or in part
- Providing office space if the librarian is to be physically colocated
- Supporting, with funding and scheduling flexibility, the librarian's continuing education in the subject domain
- Including the librarian in communications, including virtual workspaces, email lists, group meetings and events, and so forth
- Introducing a new librarian to members of the group and encouraging them to include the librarian in their work
- Meeting with the librarian, regularly or as needed, to discuss tasking and the priorities of the group and to provide feedback on the librarian's work

In the *Models of Embedded Librarianship* final report, Shumaker and Talley found that successful embedded librarians were more likely than their less-successful counterparts to benefit from these six specific management actions (Shumaker and Talley, 2009, p. 53). The extended analysis reported by Shumaker (2011b) did not find consistency in specific management actions but did find that, in all cases, management engagement in some form tended to differentiate successful from less-successful programs. Some common forms of engagement included providing support for the required continuing education and designating a member of the information user group to be a mentor or buddy to help the new embedded librarian integrate into the group.

The theme of management commitment appears repeatedly in published case studies. In one international law firm, an embedded librarian works directly for the leader of a practice group on priorities of the greatest benefit to the leader and the group as a whole, and another consults frequently with the manager of the department in which she is embedded, while also fielding requests from all members of the department. In the case of an engineering firm, the librarian meets regularly with the director of the office in which the librarian is embedded, to review progress and set priorities. In some organizations, library managers supplement these action-oriented contacts by initiating their own direct communications with the information user-group manager. These communications can take the form of a meeting or an email. They can also be informal conversations at a management meeting, as preferred by the law firm library director (Shumaker, 2011a).

The overarching point is that, whether it's formal or informal, the embedded librarianship commitment, like any other contract or commitment, should be reviewed and renewed from time to time. The library manager's job includes ensuring that the review and renewal take place, assessing the status of the relationship, and collaborating with the information user-group manager on any needed course corrections.

Problems and Pitfalls

Even when the library manager plans ahead, takes the initiative, and follows best practices, problems can arise in embedded librarianship programs. This section addresses three common problems. The first is workload management, or making sure that embedded librarians are assigned a manageable workload, with appropriate tasks, and have the support they need to avoid burnout from overwork and stress. The second is librarian collaboration and knowledge sharing: maintaining collegiality among librarians and providing opportunities for them to share experiences, get help from one another, and work together to solve common problems. The third is the continual development of staff skills, both for today's embedded librarians and for the development of staff who can step in to replace them when necessary.

Workload Management

Successful embedded librarians run a real risk of becoming victims of their success. The classic example of this is the embedded librarian who confessed to her manager that when she walked past the offices of her colleagues, she kept her head down and avoided eye contact in order to avoid getting more work to do. Similar experiences are common among embedded librarians.

Professionals are often called upon to work in excess of the standard 40-hour U.S. workweek these days—similar expectations exist in other countries—and are expected to stay connected to the office by mobile communications and computing technologies during evenings, weekends, and vacations. The expectations for embedded librarians should be no less than for others on the team. The librarian is to give the same intensity of effort as others on the team. After all, with partnership in the work team come equal expectations for effort as well as value.

The demands on embedded librarians can grow invisibly even beyond the team norms. As the information expert for the team, the librarian is presumed to be on call whenever any other member is working and needs help. If one of the librarian's tasks is to monitor the news and redistribute hot items as soon as they are available, the librarian feels pressure always to be the first with the information, no matter what time of day or night it is published. Further, as the librarian gains the trust of other team members and they begin to understand the librarian's capabilities, they identify new ways that they can benefit from the librarian's help and new kinds of tasks the librarian can perform that were not anticipated when the engagement began. Team members may not realize the impact of these new demands.

If not actively managed, growing demands can lead to disaster. Fortunately, the proactive manager who is prepared for them can be on the alert and address them as they arise.

Sometimes the librarian is asked to do work that may be inappropriate for any of several reasons. The librarian might not be the best person to perform the work because it does not leverage information management competencies. The work could be routine in nature, not at an appropriate professional level, or not very important to the team. The work might put the librarian in an awkward quasi-management position within the team and engender resentment on the part of others. All of these scenarios have happened to embedded librarians. The librarians are often reluctant to resist these demands—after all, being a member of the team also means doing whatever it takes to get the work done, and sometimes new demands can lead to growth opportunities. The astute manager, by maintaining good communication with the librarian, can sense when demands are becoming inappropriate and will intervene. This is a time when having a good manager-to-manager relationship and a clear agreement as to the librarian's role are invaluable. The library manager can discuss the concerns privately with the information user-group manager. The manager can point out discrepancies between the agreed nature of the work and repeated instances of inappropriate tasking and discuss the disadvantages of the inappropriate tasking. The challenges faced by the information user-group manager can also be explored. The best outcome of the meeting will be a renewed commitment to the original understanding or some renegotiation. In the worst case, the library manager and the librarian may have to escalate the conversation or even walk away from the engagement. When a good foundation has been laid at the outset, however, the likelihood of the worst-case outcome is very small.

When the workload management challenge has more to do with quantity than quality, a somewhat different approach is needed. In the first place, the library organization needs to remain flexible and rise to peak demands. There are times when the single embedded librarian can be seriously overwhelmed. One option, of course, is to go to the information user-group manager, discuss the situation, and negotiate priorities and expectations. It's at times like these that the manager's commitment is put to the test. The manager must be accessible and take an active role in helping the librarian manage the situation. This option should be a last resort, for it can be interpreted as showing a lack of flexibility on the part of the library manager and the librarian.

A preferred option is for the library management to provide backup for the embedded librarian. One form of backup is the ability of the embedded librarian to hand off tasks to a central library staff. Tasks such as document delivery or preliminary search and retrieval tasks are good candidates for this backup. They also provide opportunities for the central library staff to gain exposure to the work and subject domain of the information user group. Another form of backup is to establish work-sharing relationships among different embedded librarians. In an organization large enough to have several embedded librarians, it's likely everyone will have peaks and valleys in their workload—ideally at different times. Thus, there will be times when each needs help, and times when each can provide it. By formalizing the handoff process, the library manager encourages task sharing and provides opportunities for the librarians to gain insights into each other's subjects and user groups—in addition to achieving the immediate goal of providing a flexible response capability that can handle peak demands from any information user group. In one organization, library management has addressed this problem by forming *cluster groups*—informal groups of embedded librarians and other library staff members who share interest in and/or responsibilities for various specializations. The members of the cluster provide backup for one another so that the library can meet demands when a primary embedded librarian is on vacation or otherwise unavailable, as well as during peak demand periods (Trimble, 2010).

Of course, if the peak demands become chronic, and the valleys never happen, the library manager needs to get more staff. One way is to go back to the information user-group manager to renegotiate the understanding between the two. This is particularly important if the information user group is funding the embedded librarian's time. The user group needs to pay for the level of need that it actually experiences. In one case, senior librarians functioned as relationship managers with important information user organizations, such as the Marketing and Research and Development departments of the corporation. The job of the relationship manager included monitoring the amount of time and effort expended by the embedded librarians in collaborating with these organizations and negotiating funding to support the necessary staff levels. A relationship manager reported that on one occasion, her request for a doubling of the financial commitment was met with immediate agreement, and the user-group manager "responded that the InfoCenter embedded librarians were the best bargain in the company" (Shumaker, 2011a).

Librarian Collaboration and Knowledge Sharing

Libraries are warm, cozy places to work. In the traditional library setting, the librarian is surrounded by others with similar professional backgrounds who speak the same professional jargon and understand the challenges of the tasks. As a rule, there's lots of support and camaraderie. Life as an embedded librarian is very different. Almost certainly, no one else on the team has much insight into the librarian's professional challenges. This can be fun, when the members of the group view the librarian as some sort of magician who specializes in pulling information and knowledge rabbits out of a bibliographic hat. But it can also be isolating when the librarian, bereft of a peer group, has nobody to turn to for advice and support. This is not only a matter of social isolation, but also a very real lost opportunity for professional communication and knowledge sharing. In the library, librarians habitually trade insights and approaches to specific tasks, as well as knowledge of the latest innovations in tools and techniques. The embedded librarian risks losing the benefit of this professional knowledge sharing.

The wise library manager can take steps to mitigate this problem. The actions are all variations on the theme of finding ways for embedded librarians to stay connected with each other and with librarians who are still working in a centralized library.

One option is the cluster group. As described in the previous section, creating a cluster group or otherwise providing for backup and support for embedded librarians is one way to provide for workload leveling. It also helps keep the librarians connected with one another. Sharing tasks among embedded librarians or between embedded librarians and central library staff provides opportunities for them to discuss approaches, as well as new tools, techniques, and experiences that may help get the work done successfully.

The library manager can also address this concern with the information user-group manager by establishing an understanding that some small part of the embedded librarian's time—say, 10 percent—should be reserved for participation in library-related projects. In practice, it may be difficult to get the library's full share of time, but if the principle is established, then the embedded librarian can be asked to participate in library staff meetings and to contribute to library projects. In this way, the embedded librarians stay connected with one another and with the central library staff.

The tactic of getting the embedded librarian involved in central library projects has added advantages for library operations. It brings the embedded librarian's insights about the needs and behaviors of the information user group to bear on central library operations, and it can help the library to be more responsive to the information users' needs. This influence can be felt most directly in content licensing and other collection development decisions. However, it can also influence the design of library systems and services. In effect, it turns the embedded librarian into a benevolent agent of the central library, one whose unique insights can provide far better information about the community's needs than any number of surveys and focus groups could.

A final dimension of the library manager's strategy to promote librarian collaboration and knowledge sharing is the social dimension. Social interactions and relationships form the glue that holds the organization together. They contribute to trust and enable task-related collaboration to go smoothly. The importance of building the relationship between the embedded librarian and the information user group is central to this book's thesis. The same is true when it comes to maintaining the relationship of the embedded librarians with each other and the central library staff. Especially if embedded librarians are colocated with their user groups, they can be overlooked when informal lunches and other get-togethers are planned. They are out of sight and therefore out of mind. The wise library manager makes sure they are included to the greatest extent possible.

Staff Development and Succession Planning

There remains one more pitfall that the library manager must anticipate and address. Sometimes when an embedded librarian is very successful, the relationship with the information user group is strong, and the group manager is committed to its continuation, the library manager may be tempted to take a hands-off approach. After all, as the saying goes, "If it's not broke, don't fix it." The short-term risks of this approach, particularly problems of workload balancing and of disconnection between the embedded librarian and other librarians, have been mentioned already.

The longer-term danger is that the relationship may be seen as a "personal services" relationship, in which the embedded librarian is perceived by the information users as uniquely qualified and capable of performing the role. In their eyes, no one else could replace the librarian they have come to value so highly. Then something happens. The embedded librarian gets promoted, retires, or otherwise leaves the organization. The relationship, which has become highly personalized, breaks down. No successor has the knowledge, experience, or trust that the former librarian had developed, and so no successor measures up. The engagement is lost.

The wise library manager, therefore, thinks about succession in embedded roles. On a strong, well-chosen library staff, there should be candidates who have the skills and motivation to replace others in these roles. The wise manager gives them opportunities to develop, so that they are ready when the need arises.

The reader will note that the same actions recommended in the preceding sections will also contribute to developing the "bench strength" of librarians who are ready. Forming cluster groups or otherwise providing for workload sharing gives less-experienced librarians opportunities to develop their skills and understand the nature of the work. It may even give them the opportunity to gain visibility with the information user group. In this way, the information users become aware that the embedded librarian, wonderful as he or she may be, is also backed by an organization of similarly qualified professionals.

Further, collaboration on library tasks and informal socializing give the central library staff a window into the attitudes and habits of the successful embedded librarians in the organization. In these various ways, the library manager provides for the development of the library staff, prepares others to step up to embedded roles as the opportunities arise, and projects the image of the embedded librarianship program as being the product of a highly professional organization rather than the irreproducible achievement of one or two superstars.

Summary

There is an old proverb that "well begun is half done." It may contain a grain of truth, but half done is not good enough. Successful embedded librarianship requires, ultimately, leadership on the part of the manager responsible for library and information services operations.

There are specific areas in which that leadership is required.

The first is promotion. The library manager should keep up a flow of communications about the nature and achievements of embedded librarianship and should get delighted information user-group managers, senior executives, and others talking about it.

The next is ensuring that the embedded librarians are engaged in challenging work that contributes in a visible way to the work of the groups in which they are embedded. The nature of their work may call on expertise in research and analysis, instructional program development and delivery, or digital content management. The point is to align it with the needs of the group.

The third is to engage actively at the management level with the information user-group manager. Relationship management is a big part of the embedded librarian's job, but the library manager must have a role as well.

The managers should establish the terms of the relationship, and those terms should include commitments from both managers. Ongoing contacts should confirm that both are upholding their commitments. What's been created is a two-way partnership, not a one-way service delivery agreement, and both groups' commitments are critical to making it work.

Along the way, the library manager will ensure that each embedded librarian gets help when needed with workload management, stays connected with other embedded librarians and central library staff, and shares knowledge and opportunities to help other staff develop their readiness to step up to demanding embedded roles.

The library manager has one more responsibility—the evaluation of embedded librarians' work. That's the subject of Chapter 10.

References

Shumaker, D. 2011a. *Models of embedded librarianship: Addendum 2011.* Alexandria, VA: Special Libraries Association.

———. 2011b. Succeeding with embedded librarianship. *Information Outlook* 15 (4): 30–32.

Shumaker, D., and M. Talley. 2009. *Models of embedded librarianship: Final report.* Alexandria, VA: Special Libraries Association.

Trimble, J. S. 2010. Reflecting corporate strategy: MITRE's information services clusters. *Information Outlook* 14 (1): 23–25.

Chapter 10

Evaluating Your Success

In the preceding chapter, the overview of practices for success covered three of the four "habits of successful embedded librarians." It omitted one: evaluating your success. This chapter explores this fourth and final "habit" in depth.

At the beginning of Chapter 9, this factor was phrased as *ongoing service evaluation and communication of the evaluation results*. That's because it is really a combination of two distinct management actions. The first is conducting the evaluation. The second is communicating the results of the evaluation to justify continuation of the program. Clearly, it's important to evaluate the program, but the evaluation doesn't do much good if it is not used to inform management decisions about expanding, continuing, modifying, or eliminating embedded librarianship.

In the original *Models of Embedded Librarianship* analysis, several items about evaluation distinguished successful programs from less-successful ones. Two of the items that stood out were "Financial outcomes, such as Return on Investment or cost avoidance, are measured" and "Service metrics are used to justify the continuation of services." In fact, of all 22 items identified in that study as distinguishing successful from less-successful programs, these items emerged as the second- and third-most-significant differences (word-of-mouth promotion was No. 1; Shumaker and Talley, 2009).

Successful and less-successful programs differed on other items as well. The other differences included whether anecdotes about the impact of specialized services on customer work and outcomes were collected and whether research projects, documents delivered, reference questions, and training session attendance were counted. In each case, successful programs were significantly more likely than less-successful programs to use the measure. In the later, extended analysis, it was found that the two factors, use of financial measures and communication of metrics to justify embedded librarianship, were shared no matter what definition of success

181

was used (Shumaker, 2011b). No other measure of success was a consistent differentiator, but the overall finding was clear. Successful embedded librarians are more likely than others to conduct some form of evaluation of their worth. The common threads are some form of measurement activity and communication of the results to justify continuation of the embedded librarianship program.

Another important finding is that quite a variety of measures and evaluations is in use. Let's examine in more detail the options for measurement and evaluation and the factors you might consider in developing a measurement approach for your organization.

What to Measure: Activities, Outcomes, and Impacts

The measurements and evaluations mentioned in the preceding section encompass a wide range of very different elements. Some are simple counts of activities. Others, in particular anecdotes and financial measures, impart a deeper insight into the results of the embedded librarian's work. To understand these distinctions, it's helpful to think in terms of different categories of evaluation. Kotler and Lee call these *output*, *outcome*, and *impact* metrics (Kotler and Lee, 2007). In defining these categories, keep in mind that they are not rigid, precise divisions but broad, generalized groupings. In some cases, it's possible to debate the interpretation and categorization of a particular measure. However, the broad differences should become clear.

Output and Activity Metrics

Output or activity metrics tell us what you did, but they tell us very little about how well you did it. You might expand the terminology to encompass not only outputs (what you did) but also inputs (what resources you expended, in time, money, or other categories) and activities you performed. These metrics answer questions such as the following:

- How much time did you spend?
- How much did it cost?
- How many tasks did you perform?

- Did you do what was expected?
- Did you do it on time?
- Did you do it on budget?

A count of reference questions answered reveals something about the level of reference activity—but not all that much. It doesn't tell whether the questions were simple or difficult; whether the answers were full, accurate, and responsive; or whether the quality left something to be desired.

You can divide the number of questions answered by the number of hours spent by librarians doing reference work. From this, you gain some insights into workload and perhaps into efficiency. If the raw number of questions goes up or down dramatically or the number per hour of labor spent fluctuates, you may need to look more closely to determine what changes are affecting the librarians' work. However, if we are interested in assessing the value of reference services, these numbers give little insight. They don't tell whether the reference activity achieved the desired results.

Outcome Metrics

Outcome metrics begin to get at the results of your activities. They focus on the immediate, short-term results of your work and answer questions such as these:

- Did the services get used as intended?
- Were the users satisfied?
- Did you achieve your objectives?
- Did you do it well?

In traditional library reference services, for example, you might meas-ure outcomes by surveying people who have used the reference service, asking them about their satisfaction with the process. You should include a question about the relevance of the answer they received. Review selected reference transactions to gain a better understanding of the depth and complexity of requests and the completeness and accuracy of the information provided.

In a context of information literacy instruction, outcome metrics might include such things as the number of attendees (especially if the sessions are voluntary) and a comparison of scores on pre- and posttests. Pre- and posttests in particular help you gauge the effectiveness of the instructional tactics used and whether the students were able to comprehend the concepts intended to be communicated and to achieve the desired level of learning.

While outcome metrics are valuable, they still leave some very important questions unanswered. They don't tell whether your actions contributed to the achievement of long-term goals or how your efforts advanced the mission of your organization. They don't tell you whether you did the right things.

Impact Metrics

Impact metrics relate your work to the mission and strategy of the organization. They answer questions such as these:

- What was the benefit of your work?
- Did you have the right objectives?
- Did you do the right thing?

As noted in Chapters 1 and 2, the traditional model of library reference services doesn't provide many opportunities to develop impact metrics. The distance between the reference librarian's work and the mission of the organization is too great. An exception might occur if a user of reference services volunteers a thank-you to the reference librarian—and includes a description of the importance of the librarian's work on an important institutional initiative. Note that the thank-you message alone is not enough and can be considered an outcome metric at best. It's the inclusion of a message about the importance of the librarian's contribution and how it affected the organization that elevates the feedback to the status of an impact metric.

In an educational setting, where information literacy instruction is likely to be an important role of an embedded librarian, measures that associate information literacy instruction with improved student academic performance begin to give us insights into impact. If a course instructor perceives a significant improvement in the quality of student research papers when embedded information literacy instruction is provided, then evidence exists of the impact of that instruction. In one case, for instance, a university instructor noted that she could identify second-year students who had worked with an embedded librarian during their first year at the university, based on their academic performance. In other words, she perceived a lasting impact: a long-lasting educational benefit to the students from the work of the embedded librarian (Shumaker and Talley, 2009).

Applying the Framework to Embedded Librarianship

Now that we have established a framework for understanding metrics, we can apply it to the common measures found in the *Models of Embedded Librarianship* study.

Most of the measures mentioned in the introduction to this chapter fall clearly into the activity category. Counts of research projects, documents delivered, and reference questions are all activity-oriented in nature. You could debate the categorization of training session attendance counts. Are they activity measures or outcome measures? Although they tell you more than reporting just the number of sessions conducted, because they tell you how many students were exposed to the instruction, they don't tell you whether any of the students learned anything. Moreover, they surely provide no insight into the impact of the instruction on long-term academic performance.

Another commonly used measure is the collection of anecdotes about the impact of specialized services on customer work and outcomes. Its categorization is also debatable. It's more than an activity metric, but the phrase itself uses both the words *impact* and *outcomes*—so which is it? If the anecdote is limited to mentioning courteous and efficient work that allowed the group to finish its task on time, for example, then that's no more than an outcome metric. On the other hand, if the anecdote mentions contributions that were critical to the attainment of an important goal, such as launching a new product, winning a new contract, or coming up with a solution to a challenging and important technical problem, then it enters into the realm of an impact metric.

This brings us to the last metric that differentiated the successful from the less-successful programs in the initial *Models of Embedded Librarianship* study. That metric was the use of financial outcomes, such as return on investment or cost avoidance, to evaluate the program. In a for-profit organization, where financial goals are paramount, this is clearly an impact metric. If the librarian or library manager can trace a clear line from the work of the embedded librarian to the financial health of the firm, then the position of the program should be strong. In a not-for-profit organization, such as a research institute or an academic organization, the profit motive is not paramount. Instead, these organizations generally define their goals in terms of impacts on society at large. An educational institution, for example, may talk about preparing students to be effective professionals and constructive citizens. Whatever the organizational goals are, and however they are stated, the librarian's task is to implement measurements and evaluations that align with them.

Overall, it seems that successful embedded librarians employ a range of metrics, including activity, outcome, and impact measures. Each of these categories of measurement has a part to play in the sustainability of embedded librarianship. Rather than replacing one form of measurement (activity) with others (outcome and impact), however, the approach to take is one of developing measures that make sense at all levels. Generally, as noted in Chapter 2, our society is currently placing more emphasis on measurement and accountability. The implication of this trend is that outcome and impact metrics may need to be part of the mix.

The development of outcome and impact metrics can be a challenge. Activity metrics are widely collected because they are easy to collect and report. It's a harder problem to separate the impact of one factor from all the factors that go into successful organizational performance. It's even more difficult to reduce the factor's impact to a simple financial statement. There are multiple approaches to take, but a discussion of them is beyond the scope of this book. Financial impacts have been derived from time savings, savings in materials acquisition costs, and anecdotes, to name a few possibilities. Stories that illustrate impacts, or assessments of long-term impacts that relate to strategic nonfinancial measures, are equally tricky to collect and summarize. Many successful embedded librarians are continuing to experiment and develop new approaches. How high a priority to set on the development of metrics may be, above all, a matter of management culture and expectations.

Evaluation and Management Culture

As established in the preceding section, a very important reason to evaluate the performance of embedded librarianship is to justify its continuation—or expansion—in the eyes of senior executives, information user-group managers, or whoever in the organization may make or influence decisions regarding the future of an embedded librarian program. Thus, the approach to evaluation should emphasize the kinds of evaluation that will be most meaningful to the intended audience. Evaluation and communication must take into account organizational management culture, as well as personal preferences and attitudes of the key executives and managers, and must shift as their preferences change.

One very successful law firm did without a systematic evaluation of embedded librarianship (Shumaker and Talley, 2009; Shumaker, 2011a). The chief library and records officer (CLRO) pointed out that the firm did not have an accepted management practice of conducting systematic quantitative or other formal evaluations of its operations. Instead, the firm operated with a strong, open culture of communication and collaboration. The CLRO regularly attended executive-level meetings and maintained good lines of communication with the managers of information user groups in which librarians were embedded. The CLRO frequently received positive anecdotes and communications and was confident that if there were any negative feedback, it would be communicated freely and constructively. Shumaker found confirmation of this analysis in interviews with two senior managers of information user groups. Both stated that they freely praised and gave credit to the embedded librarians in their group and had shared their appreciation with the CLRO at various times. Both said that they felt no need to establish a formal mechanism for feedback and evaluation, and that if they were to have negative feedback in the future, they would not hesitate to share it.

In some situations, the approach to evaluation is driven more by personal preferences of the senior manager than by a strong corporate culture. In one unpublished and anonymous case, the members of a management team that valued descriptive measures and believed strongly in the power of anecdotes—especially those that made a clear connection between the embedded librarian's work and the success of the information user group—were all promoted or transferred to new responsibilities. Over time, their replacements introduced a more quantitative approach that emphasized activity counts. In this situation, the library manager can make the case for maintaining outcome and impact measures but ultimately must comply with the senior manager's directive.

Just as the law firm manager in the first example would be foolish to set up an elaborate tracking and reporting system that flew in the face of corporate culture, the smart manager in the second scenario will find a way to communicate with the senior manager through systematic activity counts and by the use of formal tracking systems. Regardless of the practices of successful embedded librarians across the board, each manager must above all conform to the requirements of the parent organization and the cognizant senior management.

Developing Your Evaluation Plan

The development of systematic evaluation for an embedded librarianship program is part strategy and part communication planning.

Like strategic planning, your evaluation effort should start with the ends in mind. For each metric you consider, ask what you will do with it. How will it affect the management of your program? If it goes up, or goes down, what actions might you take?

As in communication planning, consider the audience for each metric. Some measures could be for internal use by the library manager and librarians alone. Others could be intended for communication to information user-group managers or to senior managers. Some measures are valuable only for library management purposes and are not of interest to others. You don't have to use every measure in communications to stakeholders.

A library manager in a management culture that doesn't emphasize evaluation may decide to collect certain metrics anyway, as a matter of internal feedback and control. The manager may decide to keep a file of volunteered anecdotes and to encourage embedded librarians to forward the thank-you notes and kudos they receive, in anticipation of future need, perhaps due to changes in the culture. Alternatively, the library manager might decide that there is such a small likelihood of change that no metrics are necessary.

A manager working in an environment where senior management demands systematic evaluation can choose to collect a variety of metrics, including activity, outcome, and impact measures. Additionally, this manager will prepare formal reports for information user-group managers, to be used in conjunction with the management meetings discussed in Chapter 9 or distributed to senior managers. This manager will also have to figure out where the metric will come from. Who will collect it, and how? Must it be collected manually, or can it be harvested from a computer-based system already in place?

The manager who needs to collect metrics should look for opportunities to use metrics that others are already collecting for other purposes. For example, in higher education, course management systems typically keep track of the number of visits and number of postings by each participant in a course. The number of postings by an embedded librarian in the course provides an activity metric that shows the involvement level of the librarian. If there is a separate discussion thread for students to use in asking the librarian questions, the activity on that thread is an outcome metric showing the level of engagement by students in seeking the librarian's help. At the impact level, a university student tracking system could be used, with suitable privacy safeguards, to compare the academic performance of students who enroll in courses with embedded librarians early in their academic careers with the performance of students who don't enroll in those courses. A strong correlation between working with an embedded librarian and long-term success might be a very telling argument in favor of embedded librarianship. In a corporate setting, an analogous method might be tracking projects or individuals who receive corporate awards for innovation or other high-value contributions to the organization. If these projects or individuals benefited from collaboration with an embedded librarian, documentation of this fact can be a telling metric. (If the project staff is honored as a group, one would hope that the embedded librarian is included in the award!)

In any case, the overarching point is that the manager of embedded librarianship programs must think about the role of evaluation and make conscious choices about the nature and extent of evaluation that will take place.

For those who wish to document their choices, Figure 10.1 provides a worksheet.

Evaluation and Sustainability Scenarios

In this chapter and Chapter 9, I surveyed four major themes for any library manager to address in assuring that embedded librarianship will be sustainable over time:

1. Marketing and promotion
2. Delivery of sophisticated, value-added services

Measurement	Type (Activity, Outcome, Impact)	Audience and Use (Stakeholder Communication, Internal Management, etc.)	How Collected
1.			
2.			
3.			
4.			
5.			

Figure 10.1   Evaluation Planning Worksheet

3. Ongoing service evaluation and communication of the evaluation results

4. Engagement and support of library and information user-group management

Circumstances might dictate that one of these themes receive special attention at a particular time. The following exercise offers several scenarios that call for the library manager to take a certain category of sustaining action. Propose how you would address the situation. Commentary follows the scenarios.

Evaluation and Sustainability Exercise

Each of the following scenarios describes a challenge to a successful embedded library services program. Refer to concepts presented in this chapter and Chapter 10 and propose actions that the library manager should take in response to the challenge.

1. Ginormous State University's library has established a successful embedded program in which reference and instruction librarians participate in first-year speech and composition courses. The librarians' work is praised by faculty and students

alike but has never been evaluated systematically. Recently a new president has come to the university, and she has announced a new emphasis on the measurement of learning outcomes.

2. The Wise Consultants firm library has established a successful practice in which librarians are assigned to consulting engagement teams and function as full team members. Recently Wise has merged with another firm, Smart & Cleveridge, which does not have experience with embedded librarians in its consulting teams. The two library operations are to be merged under the leadership of the Wise library manager. A readiness assessment has indicated that Smart & Cleveridge librarians are ready and able to embrace embedded librarianship, but other staff coming into Wise from that firm are not yet ready to adopt it—a Quadrant 2 result.

3. The National Patent Agency has a long-established practice of embedding librarians with the departments where patent examiners with different specialties work. The primary roles of these embedded librarians are to perform "prior art" literature searching and to instruct examiners in searching techniques. Recently, the agency implemented a new, computer-based knowledge management system, In which examiners will share their analyses and decisions on applications they review. Already, the agency is encountering problems with the stewarding and management of content on the new system. A management team, which the library manager participates in, has found that the examiners do not apply proper coding to their documents—their work is often inaccurate and incomplete. The embedded librarians think they can solve this problem.

4. The embedded librarian with the intensive care department of Metropolitan Hospital is about to retire. Fortunately, she has been assisted for the past 3 years by a junior librarian, who is well prepared to succeed her in the embedded role. Still, the

junior librarian and the library manager have concerns about how the junior librarian will be integrated into the group.

Evaluation and Sustainability Exercise Comments
Case 1: Ginormous State University

In Case 1, Ginormous State University's situation is first and foremost one of evaluation, with elements of management engagement added in. There is no suggestion of extending embedded librarianship to new information user groups or changing the nature of the librarians' contribution to the university's goals and objectives, so neither marketing and promotion nor delivery of value-added work is directly involved.

If the new university president is successful in introducing systematic evaluation, the librarians should expect that their work will be subject to evaluation, too. The library manager should prepare for this change by discussing the coming change with staff and systematically listing potential metrics. The worksheet offered in Figure 10.1 may be useful for this purpose.

Because of the planning exercise, the library manager will come to see opportunities to leverage the evaluation initiatives being developed by others. The manager should form an alliance with the senior faculty or academic administrators responsible for the speech and composition courses in order to assure a unified approach to developing and measuring learning outcomes in these courses. Meanwhile, embedded librarians can monitor the attitudes and approaches of instructors and collaborate with them on evaluation methods. If the president forms a universitywide committee to develop learning outcomes and metrics, the library manager should seek a place on it. By combining planning and development of internal initiatives for the evaluation of embedded librarianship with efforts to engage information user-group managers and other stakeholders, the librarians can be well-positioned for potential changes in evaluation philosophy.

Case 2: Wise Consultants

In Case 2, the embedded librarians at Wise Consultants have a challenge that involves marketing and promotion, along with issues of management engagement on the part of library and information user-group leaders. It might seem that the obvious action would be to promote the embedded librarianship model to the staff and information user-group managers who are joining Wise from the Smart & Cleveridge organization. The library manager can use the communications planning worksheet in Figure 9.1 to list and develop the options. Everything, from making presentations at orientation sessions for the new employees to using testimonials from supportive Wise Consultant team leads in emails to Smart & Cleveridge team leads, might go on the list.

However, a strategy that relies exclusively on promotional efforts overlooks important organizational considerations, and as a result, it could well prove ineffective. The merger of two organizations can set up serious conflicts of culture and style, and the two firms' very different approaches to the role of librarians suggests that there may be other differences, as well. Since the case states that the strategy is to proceed with embedded librarianship, the library manager would do well to ensure that the library promotional efforts align with overall integration plans. For example, will employees from the two firms be combined in consulting engagement teams, or will they continue to function as largely separate entities under one management umbrella? If Wise staff and Smart & Cleveridge staff begin working together closely, then some Smart & Cleveridge staff will have the opportunity to collaborate with embedded librarians. As they gain positive experiences, they will communicate those experiences to others who have joined the firm from Smart & Cleveridge, thus generating the kind of invaluable word-of-mouth advertising that successful embedded programs often benefit from. On the other hand, it may also happen that Wise staff will be assigned to work for former Smart & Cleveridge project leaders. In those cases, the project leaders may be receptive to the new model of embedded librarianship, or they may resist. Word of mouth from their Wise team members may sway them readily, or they may require an accumulation of evidence and success stories before ultimately changing their minds later. Finally, if collaboration and interaction among the old Wise staff and the new Smart & Cleveridge personnel will be limited, then the library manager may well employ the basic communication strategy of preparing reports and holding meetings with key managers, as discussed at the beginning of the previous section, Developing Your Evaluation Plan.

The library manager's strategy should also involve the new librarians from Smart & Cleveridge. They will need orientation to the Wise organization and may need other forms of support to develop their skills or their knowledge of the subject areas that Wise works in. The formation of "cluster groups" might be a good way to develop collaboration, integrate the library staffs, and involve the new librarians in embedded engagements. At the same time, the Smart & Cleveridge librarians may be valuable assets in the promotional efforts. The library manager should take advantage of their contacts and knowledge of Smart & Cleveridge managers to identify potential partners in extending the embedded librarianship model.

Case 3: National Patent Agency

The embedded librarians at the National Patent Agency have built a strong base in information retrieval and analysis, along with information literacy instruction. The scenario provides them an opportunity to develop a new value-added role by expanding into content stewardship for the agency's knowledge management effort. The sharing of internal knowledge has become a strategic priority, the librarians have relevant expertise, and they need to volunteer to apply their skills to this high organizational priority.

The scenario indicates that the problem has to do with poor document coding. The librarians can apply their information expertise to offer several possible solutions. They could take over responsibility for coding, editing, or reviewing the content. They could offer instruction to explain the importance of accurate coding and to help the examiners do a better job of coding. They could also recommend changes to the system to make the coding process easier or to automate parts of it.

The different approaches will have differing impacts on the work of the examiners and the librarians. No matter which approach, or combination of approaches, is chosen, the librarians may have to make adjustments in their other duties to ensure that this organizational priority is addressed successfully. For example, if it is decided that the librarians will become editors and reviewers of content, they may have to spend a significant portion of their time checking the coding of documents contributed by the examiners, and making editorial changes. To do that, they may have to find new, more-efficient methods of accomplishing their other tasks. They can't assume—certainly not in the immediate future—that more staff will be forthcoming to help with the added workload. Instead, they should proactively propose changes in methods or priorities necessary to make the adjustment. In the end, they will have increased their value to the agency further by applying their information skills to a new, high-value organizational goal.

Case 4: Metropolitan Hospital

Metropolitan Hospital presents a straightforward need for engagement of the information user-group manager. The veteran embedded librarian has a strong position within the intensive care department and has involved the junior librarian to the extent that the junior librarian has good knowledge of the organizational context and subject domain of the department. The librarians have done a great deal to prepare for a smooth transition. However, it appears that there is more to be done.

So far, the intensive care department manager has not been engaged in the process. Management-level communication and commitment are needed to ensure a smooth transition. The department manager should be consulted on the transition and asked to contribute by giving the junior librarian opportunities to meet all the staff and participate in the work of the department. The department manager can either meet with the junior librarian as needed or assign another knowledgeable member of the staff to serve as a mentor for the junior librarian during the transition period. The veteran librarian can also begin to involve the junior librarian more actively, and the library manager should keep in touch with the librarians, as well as the department manager, to make sure that all is going well. The transition should be structured as a process engaging all parties.

Summary

This chapter has explored the fourth of the four habits of successful embedded librarians: evaluating their work and communicating the results of the evaluation to stakeholders who determine or influence the future of embedded librarianship in their organizations. Along the way, it analyzed different types of metrics: activity, outcome, and impact, giving examples of each, plus discussing their uses and methods of collection. The chapter also discussed the influence of organizational culture and management preference on the approach to measurement and evaluation. Before concluding with sample scenarios for analysis, the chapter offered some suggestions for tailoring evaluations to your own situation.

References

Kotler, P., and N. Lee. 2007. *Marketing in the public sector: A roadmap for improved performance.* Philadelphia: Wharton School Publishing.

Shumaker, D. 2011a. *Models of embedded librarianship: Addendum 2011.* Alexandria, VA: Special Libraries Association.

————. 2011b. Succeeding with embedded librarianship. Information *Outlook* 15 (4): 30–32.

Shumaker, D., and M. Talley. 2009. *Models of embedded librarianship: Final report.* Alexandria, VA: Special Libraries Association.

Afterword

Librarians must become "integrated parts to the whole"—they must become truly embedded in the contexts in which they work. The changes taking place in society demand that we do. The predominance of digital information has blown up the library and put it in homes, schools, dorm rooms, and offices all over the connected world—and if the library has gone out to the places where people live and work, so must the librarians. Traditional methods and modes of library service are no longer sufficient, but if librarians adopt the right new approaches, opportunities abound.

The primacy of knowledge work in developed economics of the 21st century puts a premium on information and knowledge and the skills to use them. These skills are the stock-in-trade of librarians. Adopting the embedded model can enable librarians to apply them effectively. Globalization demands adaptation, specialization, and relationship building on the part of individuals and organizations. Librarians must strengthen their own role by helping to strengthen the communities of which they are a part—embedding enables them to do this. Technical skills and rational thought processes are joined by creativity, and embedded librarians must open up opportunities to apply both right brain and left-brain aptitudes. Embedded librarians can meet the demands for transparency and accountability that are placed on everyone in modern organizations. The dominant form of community and corporate behavior is teamwork—embedded librarians must not stand apart; they must place themselves into teams as "integral parts to the whole."

Librarians are fulfilling this vision. In higher education, they are collaborating with faculty to teach information literacy skills in the classroom and online. They are partnering with researchers to find, analyze, manage, and preserve research data and scholarly content. In medical settings, informationists are ensuring that the right clinical knowledge is used by the people who need it—patients who need to understand the nature of what is happening to them, nurses who provide essential care, and doctors who must make critical decisions about diagnosis and treatment. In corporations, embedded information analysts are making everybody smarter by serving as the go-to information experts on marketing teams, research groups, design projects—anywhere in the enterprise where information and knowledge are critical to success. In schools, teacher-librarians are collaborating with classroom teachers, much as instruction librarians are doing in higher education, so that students will achieve immediate learning goals—and gain the information literacy skills that they will need throughout their lives. In communities large and small, public services librarians are reaching out to their communities and embedding themselves in community life.

In every sector, successful embedded librarians are following similar paths. They are building interpersonal relationships that enable collaboration and communication to flow freely and naturally. They are coming to grips with the ways that information and knowledge fit into what the people and the organization are trying to accomplish—not just with "information needs" in isolation. They are taking initiatives to demonstrate what they can do, and they are recruiting influential allies to help their initiatives succeed. They are making good on their promises with sophisticated professional performance that makes a difference. They are evaluating their work and sharing the news of their success in ways that conform to the culture and expectations of those to whom they are accountable. And at the same time, they are taking care of their own development and the development of other librarians in their workplaces.

As I said earlier in the book, William Gibson is routinely credited with saying that the future is already here; it's just not evenly distributed. Embedded librarians are living and creating the future of librarianship and demonstrating the skills needed to be successful there. To enter this future requires a journey and some changes along the way. If you're on this journey, planning to start out on it, or just thinking about it, I hope this book has helped you see the way forward. If you'd like to learn more, and to contribute your ideas and experiences, I invite you to join other travelers at the Embedded Librarian blog, www.embeddedlibrarian.com.

About the Author

David Shumaker has served as clinical associate professor at the School of Library and Information Science, Catholic University of America, since August 2006. Dave's teaching interests include the present and future roles of librarians in society, the management of libraries and information services, marketing, information systems, and library public services. His research and writing explore the changing roles of librarians in organizations of all types. He and his co-investigator, Mary Talley, were awarded the 2007 Special Libraries Association (SLA) Research Grant for their project, Models of Embedded Librarianship. Project documentation is available on the SLA website, and related articles have been published in *Library Journal*, *Reference & User Services Quarterly*, and *Information Outlook*. Dave is a frequent speaker and panelist on embedded librarianship.

Before becoming a full-time faculty member, Dave was a librarian at the MITRE Corporation, where he worked for 27 years. From 2001 to 2006, he served as manager of information services. In this position he was responsible for MITRE's corporate library, records management, and archives operations. Earlier in his career, he was a Library of Congress intern, a cataloger, and an automation specialist for the U.S. National Library Service for the Blind and Physically Handicapped. He holds graduate degrees from Drexel University and the University of Maryland.

Dave blogs at www.embeddedlibrarian.com.

Index

Figures and tables are indicated with f and t following the page number.

More Great Books From Information Today, Inc.

The Librarian's Guide to Negotiation
Winning Strategies for the Digital Age

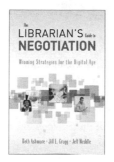

By Beth Ashmore, Jill E. Grogg, and Jeff Weddle

Librarians negotiate every day with vendors, funding agencies, administrators, employees, co-workers, and patrons—yet the art of negotiation receives little attention in library education and training. This practical guide by three experienced librarian-negotiators will help you develop the mindset, skills, and confidence you need to negotiate effectively in any situation. The authors provide an in-depth look at negotiation in theory and practice, share tactics and strategies of top negotiators, offer techniques for overcoming emotional responses to conflict, recall successful outcomes and deals gone awry, and demonstrate the importance of negotiating expertise to libraries and library careers. The result is an eye-opening survey into the true nature of negotiation—both as a form of communication and as a tool you can use to create sustainable collections and improve library service in the digital age.

264 pp/softbound/ISBN 978-1-57387-428-1 $49.50

The Accidental Health Sciences Librarian

By Lisa A. Ennis and Nicole Mitchell

Sparked by an aging baby boomer population, the dizzying pace of breakthroughs in medical research, and an unprecedented proliferation of health information, you may soon discover a career opportunity in health sciences librarianship—if you aren't already a part of this exciting field. In *The Accidental Health Sciences Librarian*, Lisa A. Ennis and Nicole Mitchell offer a thorough and up-to-date overview along with guidance on a range of critical resources, tools, and functions. Their coverage of such essential topics as HIPAA and MeSH, along with a wealth of expert tips and advice, is a must for all new, prospective, and working health sciences librarians.

232 pp/softbound/ISBN 978-1-57387-395-6 $29.50

Information Need
A Theory Connecting Information Search to Knowledge Formation

By Charles Cole

Charles Cole digs deep into the need that motivates people to search for information and articulates a theory of information need as the basis for designing information retrieval (IR) systems that engage the user's knowledge/belief system. Cole describes how such systems use signals from the user's own information environment to reduce overload, improve search results, and enhance the usefulness of information delivered on mobile devices. He explains the benefits for disadvantaged sectors of society and profiles a working system. *Information Need* is an important text for researchers and students in information science, computer science, and HCI, and for anyone interested in current IR theory, practice, and systems design.

240 pp/hardbound/ISBN 978-1-57387-429-8
ASIST Members $47.60 Nonmembers $59.50

Teach Beyond Your Reach, 2nd Edition
An Instructor's Guide to Developing and Running Successful Distance Learning Classes, Workshops, Training Sessions, and More

By Robin Neidorf

In this expanded new edition, Robin Neidorf takes a practical, curriculum-focused approach designed to help distance educators develop and deliver courses and training sessions. She shares best practices, surveys the tools of the trade, and covers such key issues as instructional design, course craft, adult learning styles, student-teacher interaction, and learning communities.

248 pp/softbound/ISBN 978-1-937290-01-6 $29.95